ENDORSEME

Few Christians understand true biblical worship. When you have this revelation, you will enter into a life-changing intimacy and love relationship with God and fulfill your destiny.

SID ROTH

Host, "It's Supernatural" Television

Pastor Shane Warren has been a cutting edge leader in church growth. This book reveals keys that unlock the ability of a local church to reach a city and region for God—and an individual to rise above his or her own difficulties. Pastor Warren's testimony that brought him from rags to riches is inspiring and faith-building.

DR. BOB RODGERS, Senior Pastor
Evangel World Prayer Center
Louisville, Kentucky

Worship seems to be the buzz word in the Kingdom of God over the past twenty years. Many books have been written on this topic, but Shane Warren's book, *Unlocking the Heavens—Release the Supernatural Power of Your Worship*, will take you into the Holy of Holies in your relationship with Christ. If you're not interested in growing closer to the Lord in your walk of faith, don't read this book. But if you are interested in drawing near to God in a more intimate way, this book is a must.

RANDY VALIMONT, Senior Pastor
Griffin First Assembly

In his latest book, *Unlocking the Heavens*, Shane Warren skillfully lays a solid foundation addressing the urgency for the church to get back in lock step with the ministry of praise and worship that was given to the church throughout the Scriptures. Warren points out that when God's people begin to praise and worship Him using biblical methods, the power of His presence comes among His people in an even greater measure. As a result, lives are transformed, drawing people into an atmosphere of intimate and lasting devotion. This book will help people understand that true worship holds the key to the throne room of the Almighty.

MARCUS D. LAMB, Founder and President
Daystar Television Network

For the past forty-one years of ministry, the fuel that has kept my personal, intimate relationship with Christ blazing has been my unceasing passion to worship. Thank God for a book that reveals this revelation to the family of God! Read it; but even greater, become the worshipper God created you to be.

PASTOR TOMMY BATES
Community Family Church
Independence, Kentucky

Pastor Shane Warren is a passionate preacher of biblical truth. In a day in which "preaching" has fallen on hard times, Shane's ministry provides a refreshing alternative. He preaches biblical truth with clarity, passion, and Holy Spirit unction. God's hand is upon him in an unusual way, which is obvious in the lives of the thousands of redeemed folks who are called "The Assembly" of West Monroe, Louisiana.

DR. SCOTT CAMP
President, Scott Camp Ministries
Dallas, Texas

Pastor Shane represents the highest level of Christian commitment. He is an excellent preacher of the Word and he genuinely loves people. He is an effective preacher of the Word of God. Without reservation I am delighted to recommend his powerful ministry!

TIM TODD, Evangelist
Revival Fires International

Shane has had tremendous success in both pastoral ministry and itinerate evangelism. His knowledge and skill as a Bible teacher is first-rate and his presentation is captivating.

JEFF ABLES
Lead Pastor, Crossroads Church
Lafayette, Louisiana

Let the worshippers arise! I believe that God has called each of us to experience Heaven on earth through our intimate worship of our Savior. In his timely and powerful new book *Unlocking the Heavens—Release the Supernatural Power of Your Worship*, author and Pastor Shane Warren brings understanding to what it truly means to worship in spirit and truth. This book is an absolute must-read for all believers. Get ready to be challenged, stirred, and compelled to go deeper in God like never before. This book is a clarion call from the throne of Heaven for true and intimate worshippers to stand firm with our worship directed to the Savior.

PATRICK SCHATZLINE, Evangelist
Mercy Seat Ministries
Author of *Why is God so Mad at Me?*

UNLOCKING THE HEAVENS

UNLOCKING THE HEAVENS

RELEASE THE SUPERNATURAL POWER OF YOUR WORSHIP

SHANE WARREN

DESTINY IMAGE® PUBLISHERS, INC.

P.O. Box 310, Shippensburg, PA 17257-0310

"Promoting Inspired Lives."

This book and all other Destiny Image, Revival Press, MercyPlace, Fresh Bread, Destiny Image Fiction, and Treasure House books are available at Christian bookstores and distributors worldwide.

For a U.S. bookstore nearest you, call 1-800-722-6774.

For more information on foreign distributors, call 717-532-3040.

Reach us on the Internet: www.destinyimage.com.

ISBN 13 TP: 978-0-7684-0377-0

ISBN 13 Ebook: 978-0-7684-8438-0

For Worldwide Distribution, Printed in the U.S.A.

1 2 3 4 5 6 7 8 / 18 17 16 15 14

CONTENTS

Chapter 1

SYMPHONY OF EARTH

Again I say to you that if two of you agree on earth concerning anything that they ask, it will be done for them by My Father in heaven (MATTHEW 18:19).

The word *agree* is the Greek word *sumphoneo;* the English equivalent is "symphony." So when we read in Matthew 18:19 that the sounds of prayer uttered in agreement by faith-filled, worshipful hearts obtain results, we have discovered one of the keys of the Kingdom of God. Heaven's light shines forth into earthly darkness because of a symphonic sound.

The word *symphony* is a compelling word, deriving from two root words: *sun* (pronounced "soon") and *phone* ("fo-nay"). *Sun* means "with," which means that more than one thing comes together. Somehow, a bridge is created and a combination results. *Phone* means a "tone or sound." The tone or sound can be made by an inanimate object such as a musical instrument, or it can be the sound of a human or heavenly voice.

In addition, another Greek word comes into play, *phaino,* which means "to cause to shine and bring forth light." In Scriptures such as the following, it is translated as "shines" or "shining":

> *And the light shines in the darkness, and the darkness did not comprehend it* (John 1:5).

> *And so we have the prophetic word confirmed, which you do well to heed as a light that shines in a dark place, until the day dawns and the morning star rises in your hearts* (2 Peter 1:19).

In other words, when there is an agreement on the earth among believers, a symphony of sound is released, and it provokes a response from Heaven. This convergence of sounds causes a breaking forth of light into the darkness of earth. I believe that this is what the Lord is doing in the earth right now, and I fervently believe that God wants my full participation as well as yours!

As I travel the nation and the world, I am seeing the convergence of sounds from every denomination, tribe, tongue, and kindred. The harmonies created by the sounds that arise from the various parts of the Body of Christ on earth are releasing a new anointing for this final hour. People are agreeing in prayer, declaring their song from one group to another, learning how to bridge the culture gap and the generation gap and to mix the tones of the worship of the people of God from every tribe and nation. These sounds release light into the atmosphere, and God shows up. God says that if any two shall agree as touching anything together in His name—whenever they can combine their anointings and release symphonic sound—He is there in the midst of them. This is a revelation!

Full-bodied worship is the key to unlocking Heaven.

WHAT IS IN THE LIGHT?

God is light: "Here is the message we have heard from Christ and now announce to you: God is light, and in him there is no darkness at all" (1 John 1:5 NCV). If He shows up, His very presence will release something. Things will happen.

What can happen when we are in symphony and when the Light shows up? I can think of three clear results, and there are more. (That's why it will take the rest of this book to explore the topic.)

1. New sounds break old cycles.

Whenever you release God's new sound, something about that sound breaks old cycles. You see, your voice does matter. That's why the psalm says, "Let everything that has breath praise the Lord" (Psalm 150:6). You have a tone that I don't have.

Did you know that there are only seven ways to mark a person's individuality? One of those seven ways is the tone of your voice. Nobody else on the face of the earth has your voice tone. An expert can pattern your speech and your voice tone and identify you by them. The other identifiers include the distinctive irises of your eye, your footprints, your handprints, your fingerprints, the texture of your hair, and of course your DNA. God put all of these markers into you, including the sound of your voice, to make you a unique individual.

The Bible tells us to use our voices to praise Him. In other words, let everything that has breath release their individual sounds. Then something will happen—God will show up.

Ephesians 5:19 and Colossians 3:16 tell us that we are to praise God in psalms, hymns, and spiritual songs. Is every song we sing a brand-new one? Not necessarily. A new sound can be a new sound on an old song. That's what the heavenly host is doing all the time. In Heaven they are worshipping by singing the songs of Moses:

> And I saw as it were a sea of glass mingled with fire: and them that had gotten the victory over the beast, and over his image, and over his mark, and over the number of his name, stand on the sea of glass, having the harps of God.

And they sing the song of Moses the servant of God, and the song of the Lamb, saying, Great and marvellous are thy works, Lord God Almighty; just and true are thy ways, thou King of saints (Revelation 15:2-3 KJV).

So the heavenly host is singing his songs, and yet, as far as we know, Moses wrote only two songs. He wrote the first song after he led the people out of four hundred years of Egyptian captivity, just before the people entered the wilderness. Moses wrote the second song just before the children of Israel were allowed to go into the Promised Land, as they were leaving the wilderness and making the transition into something new. These new songs broke old cycles. The first new song released the children of Israel from Egyptian captivity. The second new song broke the cycle of forty years of wandering in the wilderness and released the Israelites to go into the Promised Land. New sounds break old cycles.

2. New sounds release strategy.

How can you know what God wants you to do? Try releasing a new sound. We know that new sounds release strategies from Heaven, because we see it in Judges 6, the story of Gideon.

The angel of the Lord got the attention of a young man by the name of Gideon and he hailed him as a mighty man of valor. Gideon was incredulous at first, but eventually he went out at night and tore down the altars of Baal that his father had built. As soon as he had finished tearing down the altars of Baal, he built an altar to the Lord and he began to worship the Lord. He reestablished proper worship. Israel had been worshipping idols; God used Gideon to reestablish proper worship. What happened next? God had promised to tell him how to defeat the Midianites and He did. God gave him a specific and unusual strategy. He told him that he didn't need a large army, even though the Midianite army was a big one, but rather that he needed only three hundred handpicked men. Then God gave him a strategy (see Judges 7). It sounded outlandish, but the strategy included arming each of the three hundred men with an empty pitcher and a lamp. He was also supposed to give each man a trumpet. Crazy as it sounded, the strategy worked. That little band of men defeated the mighty Midianite army.

The strategy was given to Gideon only after true worship had been released. This shows how God can supply a much-needed strategy for warfare whenever God-centered worship is released. With a new sound comes a new strategy.

3. New sounds break the spirit of division.

We learn this from the same story. Gideon told his men, "Take the clay pot and the lamp and the horn. At a certain time I want you to break the pots, show your lights, and release a loud sound. By this means we will destroy the Midianites."

The name "Midianite" means strife and division. The God-ordained sound destroyed the Midianites and what they stood for. We can beat the spirit of division in our communities in the same way. By finding the sound that God wants to release in the earth, we can tear down the spirit of division between people, overcome the racism, and bring peace in the place of strife. The sound that God will give us will tear down the walls of division that separate us. It all depends on the sound.

WORSHIP IS ESSENTIAL

Worship is not about a style or place. It is primarily vertical in its focus upon the Godhead. There is more happening in worship than we could ever imagine. Powerful spiritual dynamics occur throughout worship, much more than we can perceive from our earthly perspective.

The power of pure worship provokes a response in the heavens. Did you know that the Godhead is active around the throne when worshippers offer pure, spiritual worship? That's the word picture that

Zephaniah paints for us. God sings and dances under strong emotion as He responds to His children's cries:

> The Lord your God is with you; the mighty One will save you. He will rejoice over you. You will rest in his love; he will sing and be joyful about you (Zephaniah 3:17 NCV).

In the heavens, the angels stand amazed at the Lord's response to His beloved as He releases His love songs over the Church. This is why it is so important for us to worship in the ways that bring pleasure to Him. We discover His tastes by studying the tabernacle of David. Within its humble curtains, the sounds of prayer, praise, and proclamation were being released continuously, and God responded with blessings.

God has promised to restore the power of the Davidic order of worship in the last days. Accompanying this revelation of worship will be a powerful move of the Holy Spirit in the earth that will bring in a harvest of souls.

Angels are very active during worship, and people often sense or see them in the midst of powerful worship services. Also, Jesus told us, "For where two or three are gathered together in My name, I am there in the midst of them" (Matthew 18:20). He is in our midst when we worship together.

Exodus 32:17-18 makes it clear that worship sounds like warfare to the heavens. When the people of God worship, spiritual entities assemble and do battle. Through the warfare of worship and by taking our rightful place as worship instruments, we secure the pathway to dominion. Spiritual authority is established in and through true worship. Our praise chokes off our enemies and destroys the yokes that bind us. Praise becomes a beautiful, powerful garment that replaces the spirits of heaviness and oppression.

Our worship is powerful, and we must be careful not to allow that power to be corrupted or compromised in any way. We must not betray our Lord, as did Judas, with the kiss of false worship. Every worshipper must make a priority of protecting the purity of worship through holy living and proper spiritual alignment. Those of us who are anointed as worship leaders and spiritual authorities dare not merchandise our anointing for personal gain or recognition. Spiritual leaders have a responsibility to protect our flocks from malcontents disguised as sheep who seek to rape the spiritual landscape through their merchandised worship. We will explore all of these in more depth in the chapters that follow.

THE NEW WINE IS IN THE CLUSTER

Isaiah says that the new wine is in the cluster (see Isaiah 65:8). Psalm 133 echoes this truth by stating that there is a priestly anointing released upon the unity of believers, every one of whom is part of the priesthood of all believers (see 1 Peter 2:9). Only the Levites were allowed to carry the Ark of the Covenant, and the word *Levi* means "joined." The glory of the Lord can be made fully known to the world only when the Body of Christ joins together in a harmonious way. We do not have to sing in unison, but we must sing in harmony! We can continue to be distinctive, but we must refuse to be divisive!

The Body of Christ must discover its corporate ability. Individual worship is powerfully effective; however, it is not nearly as effective as corporate worship. The Church's greatest anointing will come only when the Body of Christ, the *perfect Bride,* stands up in unity.

Streams of ministry are converging for such a time as this to release the sound of Heaven in the earth. I have found that when sermons cannot get people together, a song can. I know that worship will be one of the essential unifying factors for the Church in the last days. The Church will discover and unleash new sounds so that "...the manifold wisdom of God might be made known by the church to the principalities and powers in the heavenly places" (Ephesians 3:10). A convergence of Heaven and earth is taking place right now! The Kingdom is coming to earth as it is in Heaven. God has always chosen to do His finest work through His Church. We, the Body of Christ, must prepare ourselves for God's final agenda in the earth.

Worship is a powerful weapon in the arsenal of the believer. On the wings of worship, you can take heavenly flight with the angels around the throne where you will discover the innumerable facets of God's unspeakable glory. The greatest desire in the heart of God is to be known by the men and women He has created. Our greatest need is to know God. Worship—the most natural thing in the world for the Christian and the reason for our creation—is the vehicle of intimacy. It always has been, and it always will be.

Listen! Can you hear the sound of Heaven? Raise your voice and join in!

Chapter 2

THE POWER OF SOUND

O come, let us sing unto the Lord: let us
make a joyful noise to the rock of our
salvation. Let us come before his presence with
thanksgiving, and make a joyful noise unto
him with psalms (PSALM 95:1-2 KJV).

You may think that worship and praise is just us standing there "aweing" God. But it's much more than that. Worship is *loud*. It's filled with all kinds of sounds. Together those blended sounds make up a "new song" of perpetual praise to our God.

In the first chapter, I introduced the idea of agreement (*sumphonio*) in prayer and worship. God likes what He hears when two or more people make a harmonious appeal to Heaven, because their worship has been inspired by God in the first place. Their divinely combined voices guarantee a heavenly response.

Look again at Matthew 18:19. Here are Jesus' words: "Again I say to you that if two of you agree on earth concerning anything that they ask, it will be done for them by My Father in heaven." In other words, if the right sound of two or more people coming together mixes and blends and releases a symphony into the atmosphere, a corresponding release takes place in the heavens; God acts on behalf of the worshipping people who are part of His Kingdom on earth. James wrote, "Draw nigh to God, and he will draw nigh to you" (James 4:8 KJV). You *draw nigh* with the release of a sound. Earth has to make a sound before Heaven will respond.

THE SOUNDS OF THE TABERNACLE OF DAVID

David's tabernacle stood for forty years in Israel. It was a place of worship, a tent housing Moses' Ark of the Covenant, and King David set it up right on Mount Zion (Jerusalem). Moses had instituted a worship system in his tabernacle that involved animal sacrifices, but David substituted "sacrifices of praise"—joyful songs of thanksgiving. Day and night for four decades, a new sound of worship was released heavenward from the tabernacle of David. Eventually, David's son Solomon moved the tabernacle into his newly built temple (see 2 Chronicles 5–7).

David's tabernacle did not keep people out as Moses' tabernacle had done with its Outer Court, Holy Place, and Holy of Holies. Instead, the people of Israel could come and go twenty-four hours a day. Following David's initiative, no longer were the priests the sole proprietors of the priestly functions of making offerings. Now all could worship freely, making their sacrifices of praise. They worshipped with their voices, even choirs of voices. They played stringed instruments. Trumpets blared. Shouts rang out. After David died, some of the subsequent kings (the ones who were righteous, starting with his son Solomon) further established Davidic worship. They were rewarded by a response from Heaven in the form of repeated spiritual renewal and military victories.

The Davidic style of worship is now the pattern, not only for those of the post-Davidic Old Testament era, but also, as James explained to the early church, for all New Testament believers, including you and me. James, quoting the prophet Amos, explained in Acts 15:13-18 how the Davidic order of worship would become normative. He quoted as follows:

> *On that day I will raise up the tabernacle of David, which has fallen down, and repair its damages; I will raise up its ruins, and rebuild it as in the days of old* (Amos 9:11).

Isaiah 16:5 and Amos 9:11-12 refer to the tabernacle of David by name. Any time we read Old Testament prophecies about Zion, the mountain of the Lord, or often, the glory of the Lord, the prophecy concerns Davidic worship because it refers to the coming Messianic Kingdom.

The New Testament authors picked up the same theme, quoting and echoing the Old Testament. John wrote that Jesus had tabernacle-damong us (John 1:14). The new Church is called the temple of God (see 1 Corinthians 3:16; Ephesians 2:19-22). The Church maintained the Davidic form of worship—noisy, heartfelt, corporate worship. Dating from the Pentecost when the Holy Spirit was given to the Church, boisterous worship increased. (See Acts 2. Remember, the bystanders thought the believers were drunk!)

The Psalms are a collection of prayers and songs that were used in the original Davidic worship. Some of them came with musical instructions. Psalm 7, for instance, is called "A shiggaion of David which he sang to the Lord about Cush, from the tribe of Benjamin":

> *Lord my God, I trust in you for protection. Save me and rescue me from those who are chasing me. Otherwise, like a lion they will tear me apart. They will rip me to pieces, and*

no one can save me. Lord my God, what have I done? Have
my hands done something wrong? (Psalm 7:1-3 NCV)

A prayer or a psalm known in Hebrew as a *shiggaion* is meant to be sung in a wild and frenzied manner. *Shiggaion* comes from the verb *shagah,* which means "to reel about through drink." When lyrics are set upon *shigionoth*, they have been written according to various tunes and were (according the *Illustrated Bible Dictionary*) "composed under strong mental emotion; songs of impassioned imagination accompanied with suitable music." Apparently, David sometimes said, "Okay, in order for us to really praise God here, I need you to go wild and be frenzied."

Often, church is entirely too dignified. Sometimes, like David, we need to get really undignified before God. Other times, we need to calm down in response to the Spirit. *Higgaion* or *Haggion, Selah,* means, "Resonate that note," "Pause for meditation for longer than normal," or "Think about it." The words appear in the midst of the ninth Psalm:

> *The nations have fallen into the pit they dug. Their feet are*
> *caught in the nets they laid. The Lord has made himself*
> *known by his fair decisions; the wicked get trapped by what*
> *they do. Higgaion. Selah. Wicked people will go to the grave,*
> *and so will all those who forget God* (Psalm 9:15-17 NCV).

Meditation allows for the times when people come into the presence of God and just begin to hum or groan as they circle their thoughts around what has been sung.

In the ebb and flow of effective worship, people must respond to the leading of the Spirit of God.

HOW TO EXPRESS OUR WORSHIP TO GOD

We need to quit letting people in the balconies control what we think or how we express our worship to God. Have you ever noticed that it's the people who never participate in the glory of God who are always the observers, never part of the action, often too critical of people who have a spirit of worship on them? That's how David's wife Michal reacted when her husband danced before the Lord when the ark was first brought back into Jerusalem:

> *And David danced before the Lord with all his might; and David was girded with a linen ephod. So David and all the house of Israel brought up the ark of the Lord with shouting, and with the sound of the trumpet. And as the ark of the Lord came into the city of David, Michal Saul's daughter looked through a window, and saw king David leaping and dancing before the Lord; and she despised him in her heart. And they brought in the ark of the Lord, and set it in his place, in the midst of the tabernacle that David had pitched for it: and David offered burnt offerings and peace offerings before the Lord. And as soon as David had made an end of offering burnt offerings and peace offerings, he blessed the people in the name of the Lord of hosts* (2 Samuel 6:14-18 KJV).

When Michal criticized David for his spirit of worship and his *shiggaion*, his frenzied outbreak in nothing but a skimpy linen garment, dancing in worship through the streets of Jerusalem, she said, "Are you crazy? A king shouldn't be acting like this."

How did he respond? He didn't say, "Well, dear, you are right, you know. As a king, I need to be a little more dignified; I need to wear my suit a little tighter." Instead he said—still caught up in the spirit of worship—"You had better watch out, Honey, because if you think I've been undignified down there in the street, I am fixing to lose my mind up in the temple worshipping God." And he began to throw off his kingly robes again.

NO SUCH THING AS SILENT PRAISE

Not that we should throw off our clothes every time we worship in church; there are a lot of ways to praise the Lord. We can't box God in to only one form of praise. Of one thing I am sure: *there is no such thing as a silent praise.* Praise has to release a sound, or it is not praise. Every posture of praise involves releasing some kind of sound.

Take the example of Psalm 95, which is quoted at the beginning of this chapter: "O come, let us sing unto the Lord: let us make a joyful *noise* to the rock of our salvation, and make a joyful *noise* unto him with psalms."

And don't forget Isaiah's *shaggaion:*

> *Sing to the Lord a new song, and His praise from the ends of the earth…Let the wilderness and its cities lift up their voice…Let the inhabitants of Sela sing, let them shout from the top of the mountains. Let them give glory to the Lord, and declare His praise in the coastlands* (Isaiah 42:10-12).

Not only does every posture of praise involve releasing some kind of sound but also every sound that we utter in praise and worship brings us nearer to God. Remember what James wrote: "Draw nigh to God and he will draw nigh to you." To draw nigh means to draw near. We reach out to Him as a bride reaches out toward her husband on their wedding day. Naturally, he reaches back, and the two begin to dance together.

When we lift our voices in praise and worship, Heaven opens up to us. God says, "I want this dance with you, My Bride. You and I are dancing. You are matching My steps." After a while, He may lean down to your ear and whisper some secrets or some endearments to you, just as a bridegroom might do with his beloved. He responds and she responds. It's an intimate, heavenly dance, although we do not have to wait until we get to Heaven to dance a heavenly dance.

So in our worship of God, we release that special sound. That sound creates a melody, a dance in our spirit. That is the reason the Bible says, "be filled with the Spirit; speaking to one another in psalms and hymns and spiritual songs, singing and making melody in your heart to the Lord," (Ephesians 5:18-19). A melody is released with sound. You start dancing, and the next thing you know something heavenly takes place. Heaven responds and comes down and starts dancing with you. All of a sudden, you can feel the presence of God.

DAVIDIC WORSHIP IN THE NEW TESTAMENT

The New Testament is filled with instructions about prayer and praise. For example:

> *...be filled with the Spirit; speaking to yourselves in psalms and hymns and spiritual songs, singing and making melody in your heart to the Lord* (Ephesians 5:18-19 KJV).

> *Let the word of Christ dwell in you richly in all wisdom; teaching and admonishing one another in psalms and hymns and spiritual songs, singing with grace in your hearts to the Lord* (Colossians 3:16 KJV).

> *So what should I do? I will pray with my spirit, but I will also pray with my mind. I will sing with my spirit, but I will also sing with my mind* (1 Corinthians 14:15 NCV).

> *So, I want the men everywhere to pray, lifting up their hands in a holy manner, without anger and arguments* (1 Timothy 2:8 NCV).

So through Jesus let us always offer to God our sacrifice of praise, coming from lips that speak his name (Hebrews 13:15 NCV).

By the time we get to the book of Revelation, we can see that worship is louder than ever. In scene after scene, John describes heavenly worshippers shouting (see Revelation 19:1), exclaiming "Alleluia!" (see Revelation 19:1-6), standing up and then throwing themselves prostrate (see Revelation 4:10), as well as "singing a new song" (Revelation 5:9). In Heaven, this goes on and on and on, without ceasing. When we pray and worship, we are joining not only with a heavenly choir but also with a heavenly ruckus.

Remember what happened on the day of Pentecost when 120 faithful believers were gathered in an upper room, waiting and worshipping (see Acts 2). Suddenly, the room was filled with the sound of a mighty rushing wind, a sound from Heaven that swept through the whole place even though the doors were shut. Then cloven tongues of fire rested on their heads individually, and they began to speak out in many languages—so raucously that the people in the street below could hear them.

It was as if the wind of the Spirit started blowing on them to the point that they began to resonate with the noise. You know how it is when you blow across the mouth of a bottle or rub a wet finger around the lip of a crystal vessel. The sound waves that result from the applied pressure become audible to the human ear.

When the Church worships, Heaven begins to resonate with earth. God Himself begins to woo His Bride and to dance with her. His Spirit fills her to the point that she must express herself in an audible way. Her profuse expressions of endearment and delight build into even more worship. She can hear John, Jesus' beloved disciple, saying, "I heard, as it were, the voice of a great multitude, as the sound of many waters and as the sound of mighty thunderings, saying, 'Alleluia! For the Lord God Omnipotent reigns! Let us be glad and rejoice and give Him glory, for the marriage of the Lamb has come, and His wife has made herself ready'" (Revelation 19:6-7).

Even now, make a joyful noise unto the God of our salvation!

Chapter 3

WHEN AN ALTAR
BECOMES A WELL

*So He came to a city of Samaria which is called
Sychar, near the plot of ground that Jacob gave to
his son Joseph. Now Jacob's well was there. Jesus
therefore, being wearied from His journey, sat thus by
the well. It was about the sixth hour* (JOHN 4:5-6).

My father, who once was a very successful entrepreneur, became very
ill and never got better. As a result, he died a pauper. Most of the first
part of my adult life, I watched my hero suffer terribly at the hands of
physicians, only to lose the battle at the age of fifty-seven. On the heels
of his death, my mother, who had taken care of him for over eighteen
years, was overcome by grief and illness as well. She too died at the age
of fifty-seven, three years after my father's death, literally dying a slow
and awful death of starvation from medications and grief. In the final

months of her life, my brother and I took turns trying to help pull her out of the clutches of the grave. At one point she was staying in our home under hospice care.

Those were definitely the saddest days of my life. At night I slept restlessly, often soaking my pillow with tears. Night after night before I tried to sleep, I lay next to my mother, trying to bring her some comfort. With my arms wrapped around her frail, sixty-pound body, I would plead with God for her health and life. At that time I could not talk about her condition with other people; we could not have much fellowship because my mother was so uncomfortable with groups.

Late one night, literally at the end of my emotional, physical, and financial rope, I got up out of bed at 10:30 p.m. and went to a small room in our home where I kept an electric guitar. I have always wished I could play well, but I am not very good. Putting the guitar strap around my neck, I said these words to God, "God, I don't blame You for my mother's condition. I don't understand. I am a man of faith and prayer. Many times I have laid my hands on people and have seen them instantly healed. I have watched blinded eyes open in my services and observed deaf ears miraculously hear. I have prayed and believed for my mother, and now I am empty. There are no more words for prayer and supplication. The only thing I have left is my song of worship, and I refuse to let Satan or any questionable circumstances take that! So, tonight I am going to turn this amp up and play unto You because I don't have anything else to give."

As I began to play, I could feel the presence of God invading the atmosphere of my house, especially in that little room. At one point I lost track of time and place and felt as if I were being carried to the high places of the earth. I thought of Deuteronomy 32:13 (KJV), which reads, "He made him ride on the high places of the earth, that he might eat the increase of the fields; and he made him to suck honey out of the rock, and oil out of the flinty rock."

Out of the heavenlies came joy that replaced my sorrow and strength that replaced my weakness. Unfathomable peace took hold of my mind as the glory of God like a cloud enveloped me. What came to my mind was the Scripture stating that when Jesus' temptation had ended, "angels came and ministered to Him" (Matthew 4:11). I could physically feel the resources of Heaven making deposits in my bankrupt soul.

Eventually I came to myself again, and I was still sitting in my chair in that room with my guitar hanging from my neck. The clock read 6 a.m. For almost seven hours, I had been translated into a different realm as the Lord had ministered to me. My weakest moment had been transformed into fresh strength.

ALTAR OF WORSHIP BECOMES A WELL OF RESOURCE

The next morning as I joined my staff in prayer at 9 a.m., I inquired of the Lord, "What happened last night?" He gently whispered to my spirit, "You built an altar of worship to Me, and I made it a well of resource for you."

From that day forward, I have made my way nightly into that little secret place and soared into the heavenlies on the wings of worship. Since that time there have been more sad, lonely, hard days. However, each time I build the altar of worship, my strength is renewed, my fears are swept away, and I receive numerous revelation keys that unlock the heavens over my life and ministry. From that initial experience, I have found many resources at the *well of worship*. The Lord's words to me, "You built an altar of worship to Me, and I made it a well of resource for you," resonated even more when I realized their significance in the context of one of Jesus' encounters—the meeting with the Samaritan woman at the well.

Here's the story. The Lord Jesus, walking from place to place with His disciples, decided to go through a region called Samaria. Because the Pharisees were trying to incite competition between Jesus and John the Baptist (see John 3:25-30), Jesus had left Judea and started north for Galilee, where He spent over eighty percent of His ministry time. He could have taken several routes to arrive at His destination: along the coast, across the Jordan and up through Perea, or straight through Samaria. These routes were well-traveled and well-known in Jesus' day.

However, Orthodox Jews almost always avoided Samaria because of a long-standing, deep-seated hatred for the Samaritan people. The Samaritans were a mixed race—part Jew and part Gentile. During the Assyrian captivity of the ten northern tribes in 727 B.C., Jews and Gentiles had intermarried and naturally produced offspring. Because of their captivity, many could not subsequently prove their genealogy. Thus, they were rejected by Orthodox communities. At that time Samaritans established their own temple and religious services at Mount Gerizim. This development aroused even greater animosity against the Samaritan people because, to the Orthodox Jews, they appeared to be insulting the temple services of Jerusalem. The fires of prejudice were so great toward the Samaritan people that Pharisees would actually pray that no Samaritan would be raised in the resurrection. A Jew was considered unclean if he had the dust of Samaria on his feet! In fact, when the enemies of Jesus wanted to insult Him and His ministry they called Him a Samaritan (see John 8:48).

The wonderful thing about Jesus is that He was never controlled by the cultural restrictions of the day. Instead, most of His actions were completely countercultural for that era. He was motivated by His unchanging, overwhelming love and compassion to reach into people's lives, even when those lives had been wrecked by the people's own wickedness. Jesus had a remarkable ability to reach across racial, religious, and socioeconomic lines. This ability made and continues to make Him relevant to every generation. Contrary to what popular critics assert, Jesus has never had a problem being relevant to the world; He is "the same yesterday, and today, and forever" (Hebrews 13:8).

Jesus arrived at the well at the sixth hour (about twelve noon). This was not the normal time for women to fetch water, which was either early in the morning or late in the afternoon. The disciples went into town to buy supplies while Jesus waited at the well. The Scripture says specifically that Jesus was weary from the journey and sat down on Jacob's Well: "Now Jacob's well was there. Jesus therefore, being wearied from His journey, sat thus by the well: and it was about the sixth hour" (John 4:6). It was there that He encountered a woman whose life desperately needed a healing touch.

Before getting any deeper into this story, a little-known truth about Jacob's well must be established. Genesis 12:5-7 (KJV) records the following:

> *And Abram took Sarai his wife, and Lot his brother's son, and all their substance that they had gathered, and the souls that they had gotten in Haran; and they went forth to go into the land of Canaan; and into the land of Canaan they came. And Abram passed through the land unto the place of Sichem, unto the plain of Moreh. And the Canaanite was then in the land. And the Lord appeared unto Abram, and said, Unto thy seed will I give this land: and there builded he an altar unto the Lord, who appeared unto him.*

God had promised Abram (Abraham) a land; and as he moved into the land, he came to a place called Sichem (also known as Sychar). It was at Sichem that God confirmed His promise to Abraham; so Abraham built an altar to worship God there. It is interesting that Sichem is not mentioned at all in the life of Isaac, Abraham's son; rather it was mentioned in Jacob's life. Jacob was Abraham's grandson. The Scripture skipped a generation. Then, in Genesis 33:18-20, we read that Jacob came to Sichem. There he built another altar.

Then we read in Joshua 24:32 that Joseph, Jacob's son, was buried in Shechem—which is the same place as Sichem—in a parcel of ground that Jacob bought for one hundred pieces of silver. Thereafter, the name Sicham, Shechem, or Sychar, is mentioned numerous times throughout the Old Testament. Then, in the New Testament, we read about Jesus' encounter with the Samaritan woman: "Then cometh he to a city of Samaria, which is called Sychar, near to the parcel of ground that Jacob gave to his son Joseph. Now Jacob's well was there" (John 4:5-6 KJV).

The altar that Abraham had built when he first came to Sichem had evolved into much more than an altar. Fresh water had been found under the ground and a strong well had been built to serve generations of travelers and the people who had their dwellings nearby. Everyone knew it as Jacob's Well. In other words—and this is significant—the altar that Abraham had built had become a well of resource.

The fact that Abraham built an altar of worship created an opportunity for a much later generation to be resourced by revelation. Now, with Jesus' visit, the well became not just a place to draw water; it was a place of worship again! This portrays one of the most powerful principles that you can ever learn: worship is a mighty resource.

In fact, you can find this secret within the word *worship* itself. The origins of the English word *worship* come from the Anglo-Saxon compound word *weorthscype*. The first syllable, *weorth*, means "worth, value, or respect," and scype means "to shape or to build." Therefore, worship is by definition the creation of worth, value, and respect.

Worship is vital because it builds something important. We see it again when we read: "You sit as the Holy One. The praises of Israel are your throne" (Psalm 22:3 NCV). When we worship, we are building God a seat to sit upon! Just as the Ark of the Covenant provided a Mercy Seat for God to sit upon, so also our praise creates a place for Him to sit. He exercises His merciful authority from that praise-built throne.

Jesus spoke to the woman and persuaded her that He was the Messiah. She summoned the whole town to come and see him. (See John 4.) Before the day was over, Jacob's Well was providing much more than plain water—it had become a source of living water.

———

In the chapters of this book, I will reveal the secrets that I have found at the well with the Lord. You will find some keys woven into the pages of this book that could very well turn your life around to the glory of God and unleash the abundance of Heaven on your behalf. Why not start now? Before you read another word, simply take the next fifteen to thirty minutes to worship. Before you finish this book, find a quiet place, lift your voice, and open your heart, and start to worship. I am asking God to give you and your fellow readers the same throne room experience that I have had so many times.

Build the altar of worship! That is where you will find all of the resources you need. You cannot find your resources in human strength. They can be found only as you soar to the high places of the earth through worship. Allow the wings of your worship to use the winds of your turmoil to take you out of this troubled earthly atmosphere into the abundance of a heavenly one.

Chapter 4

SECRETS OF THE WELL

A woman of Samaria came to draw water. Jesus said to her, "Give Me a drink." ...Then the woman of Samaria said to Him, "How is it that You, being a Jew, ask a drink from me, a Samaritan woman?" For Jews have no dealings with Samaritans (JOHN 4:7,9).

When Jesus encounters the Samaritan woman drawing water in the middle of the day, which is highly unusual, we quickly learn from their conversation that there are probably some good reasons for her timing. Normally, she would go the well to fetch water in the middle of the day to avoid the scrutiny, rejection, and even mockery of the other women. As Jesus noted, she was far from being an expert on relationships, having suffered the pain of five divorces and currently living out of wedlock with a sixth man. In all likelihood, she did not come to the well when the others did because her lifestyle had shamed her before the other women of the community. Perhaps she could not take any more of the other women's questioning her about her serial relationships in a society that highly valued monogamy. She had run out of explanations, and the less said, the better. Her current lifestyle was her own business. Besides, every time the subject came up, the wounds of relationships gone bad were reopened just as botched surgeries that can never heal. The oppression of past failures and reproach for her current questionable lifestyle enforced a penalty of isolation and inconvenience. Trips to the well in the heat of the day were only part of the picture.

Today she could not retrieve her supply of water without being noticed. What was this Jewish man doing here? As He asked for a drink, His tone of voice did not seem to indicate any hint of the traditional antagonism between the Jews and the Samaritans.

FROM NATURAL WELL TO HEAVENLY WELL

Jesus' prophetic eyes must have seen a desire for breakthrough in the heart of this woman. I must admit that of all of the people in the Bible, a woman of her character would not have been my personal choice of someone to whom to reveal the greatest revelation about worship in the New Testament; however, "the Lord does not see as man sees; for man looks at the outward appearance, but the Lord looks at the heart" (1 Samuel 16:7). In His mercy, the Lord gave this nameless Samaritan woman a key that would change her life, heal her brokenness, and remove her shame—the key of worship.

Right away, the conversation took an interesting turn. No sooner did He reveal her deepest secrets and thus prove that He was more than just another thirsty traveler, than He immediately started teaching her about worship. There, sitting on the edge of Jacob's Well, which long before was an altar of worship, He revealed to a woman who had come to draw her day's water from a natural well how to find the ever-renewable resource of a heavenly well. Worship was the key.

This woman's life was in a mess. No amount of well water could wash her clean or satisfy her thirst for love. While Jesus knew that worship would restore and heal her devastated life, she could not understand at first. He needed to talk about true worship. The problem was this woman's concept of worship had been skewed by the deep-seated cultural hatred between the Jews and her people. In order to position her to receive all of what He wanted to show her, Jesus first had to explain three common fallacies about worship.

FALLACY NUMBER ONE: YOU MUST WORSHIP IN THE RIGHT PLACE

The Samaritan woman said, "Our fathers worshiped on this mountain, and you Jews say that in Jerusalem is the place where one ought to worship" (John 4:20). She was making the same mistaken assumption that many church people do today—that worship must occur in a certain place, or that worship is something that happens only on Sunday mornings, Sunday nights, and Wednesday nights. We Christians have erected great shrines to mark our places of worship.

In reality, worship transcends place. In fact, it has little to do with a place, but everything to do with a Person. You could even say that assigning worship only to a particular place is a form of idolatry.

The human race has a tendency toward idolatry, but sometimes it is hard to see. For example, consider the idolatry that Hezekiah opposed. (See 2 Kings 18.) As one of the righteous kings who came after King David, Hezekiah had his work cut out for him. He became king at twenty-five years of age, and his first act as king was very unusual. Did he erect a monument to his father or try to improve the economy? No. His first act as king was to reestablish true worship in Israel.

Second Kings 18:1-8 records the following things King Hezekiah did to refocus the people in true worship:

- He removed high places.

- He broke the images.

- He cut down the groves.

- He broke in pieces the brazen serpent of Moses.

The people at this time were steeped in idol worship, and yet it is interesting to note that some of the things Hezekiah destroyed were *not* dedicated to idols, but rather to the worship of God. The brazen serpent of Moses had been fashioned according to the instruction of God for the healing of the people of Israel after they were bitten by serpents (see Numbers 21). This was a God-ordained, sacred object, so why would he destroy it? For the simple reason that the people had made it into an idol. They had started offering incense to something that God had once used, but they were not really looking to God Himself. Anytime our worshipful attention gets directed toward an object, a methodology, or a place instead of God, it becomes idolatry.

Several years ago, I was trying to help a church that was experiencing a split. The conflict had started because they were renovating the sanctuary to accommodate more growth. A certain group within the church was against the renovation project because it altered their "sacred" sanctuary. In prayer, I was rebuking the devil of division in this church when the Lord interrupted me: "This isn't the work of the devil; this is Me."

I said, "Lord, I don't understand. How can this be Your work?"

He replied, "This group of people has made this place more important than Me. It must be destroyed or others will be swept into their idolatry. Sometimes I have to pull down and destroy so that I can build."

Please do not misunderstand; I strongly believe in the importance of corporate gatherings in houses of worship. I love the local church—I am a pastor! Clearly, however, we have to avoid the belief that *church* means a place, a building. We are the Lord's body, and we carry His presence everywhere we go. True worshippers enjoy the presence of God in their home, at work, or on vacation.

When King David desired to build God a house, God told him, "I never told you to build me a house (paraphrased from 2 Samuel 7:4-12). Then God promised David, "I will build *you* a house…" (see verse 27). In essence, God was saying to David, "I don't want a place in which to dwell. I am looking for a people in whom to dwell." Jesus stated this same principle to the Samaritan woman when He told her, "Believe me, woman. The time is coming when neither in Jerusalem nor on this mountain will you actually worship the Father" (John 4:21 NCV).

FALLACY NUMBER TWO: YOU MUST WORSHIP IN THE RIGHT WAY

To the woman's understanding, Jesus' response was based on a similar false assumption. He said, "You worship what you do not know; we know what we worship, for salvation is of the Jews" (John 4:21-22). Her concept of true worship was based on her cultural understanding. She knew that Jews worship one way and that Samaritans worship another. Her form of worship seemed best to her because it was all she knew.

How many worship wars are started over the issue of style? What is the most anointed style of worship, Southern Gospel or Contemporary? How many times do we hear statements such as, "I wish we had the old red-backed hymnals back," or "When are we going to start putting the lyrics up on a screen?" I had just started pastoring when churches first discovered the overhead projector. My parishioners felt I had committed the unpardonable sin when I removed the hymnals so we could sing from overheads. Sometimes worship wars are frivolous!

"Worship is not about the song that you sing, but the heart that you bring!" It has been my good fortune to travel the world preaching the Gospel. I have ministered in the remotest parts of Africa where pots, pans, and drums were the only musical instruments available. That's where I have heard some of the most anointed worship in the world. Those people are not preoccupied with equipment, lights, or styles. They are preoccupied with Jesus. During my most recent trip to Nigeria, the worship was so anointed that hundreds of people manifesting demons were delivered—through the power of worship alone. They did not have hymnals or projectors and screens, high-quality musical instruments or trained vocalists. They were just people bringing to God their hearts of worship.

Worship transcends style. When we get to Heaven, we will see every style of worship because we will see every tribe, tongue, kindred, and nation in full demonstration around the throne. It is foolish to expect everyone to abandon his or her cultural style in favor of the red-backed hymnal. If you are offended to think that your favorite worship style is being threatened, it could be that God is trying to give you a secret from the well of worship. I happen to love Southern Gospel music above all other types (and I am convinced that God loves it too). However, in my church we sing mostly contemporary songs. Why? We decided to use the style of music that inspires this current generation to worship. Real, biblical worship is the blending of many styles; "psalms, hymns, and spiritual songs" (Ephesians 5:19; Colossians 3:16).

FALLACY NUMBER THREE: GOD WANTS OUR WORSHIP

How can this be a fallacy? Of course God wants our worship... doesn't He? At the risk of sounding sacrilegious, I must tell you that in fact, God is not the least bit interested in our worship. Let me explain.

Look at Jesus' statement to the Samaritan woman: "the hour is coming, and now is, when the true worshippers will worship the Father in spirit and truth; for the Father is seeking such to worship Him" (John 4:23). Jesus has already shown her that worship is not about place or style. Now He deals with worship itself. He knows that people believe God wants our worship. Here is the truth: God is not looking for worship; He is looking for *worshippers!*

Worship is something that you do, but a worshipper is who you are. Worship is an act, but being a worshipper is a lifestyle. That's why worship does not take place only on certain days and according to certain rituals. The heart of worship should be churning within us continuously. "Therefore by Him let us continually offer the sacrifice of praise to God, that is, the fruit of our lips, giving thanks to His name" (Hebrews 13:15).

Worship is an issue of the spirit. "God is a Spirit: and they that worship him must worship him in spirit and in truth" (John 4:24 KJV). Real worship is more than an act; it is a connecting of spirits. In fact, God is not at all pleased when we perform the act of worship apart from a life of worship. The prophet Samuel rebuked Saul, saying, "Has the Lord as great delight in burnt offerings and sacrifices, as in obedience to the voice of the Lord? Surely, to obey is better than sacrifice, and to heed than the fat of rams" (1 Samuel 15:22 NRSV).

The Bible tells us that God is always looking for true worshippers: "For the eyes of the Lord range throughout the entire earth, to strengthen those whose heart is true to him" (2 Chronicles 16:9 NRSV). Are you one of those people? Are you a true worshipper, or are you someone who just goes through the motions of worship on Sundays? What can you do to become a true worshipper? How can we grow out of our faulty assumptions about worship? How can we respond to the Lord's love? What does it mean to spend time with Him? Too many of us are like the Samaritan woman; we worship, but we do not know the One we are worshipping.

—◦◦◦—

Jesus has just stopped by to teach us the secrets of the well of worship. Let's spend some time with Him.

Chapter 5

A SONG IN THE NIGHT

Because of the multitude of oppressions they cry out; they cry out for help because of the arm of the mighty. But no one says, "Where is God my Maker, who gives songs in the night? (JOB 35:9-10)

Theology (the study of God) used to be called the Queen of Sciences because it deals with the most important knowledge of all—the knowledge of God. Theology is important, yet it is the most difficult kind of science because in many ways theologians are trying to explain what is unknowable. The Bible says, "Oh, the depth of the riches both of the wisdom and knowledge of God! How unsearchable are His judgments and His ways past finding out!" (Romans 11:33).

On the other hand, although God is unknowable, He has revealed Himself in many ways. The most basic way we can see Him is in His creation. We are familiar with the words of the Bible: "The earth is the Lord's and the fullness thereof" (Psalm 24:1 KJV). "The heavens declare the glory of God; and the firmament shows His handiwork" (Psalm 19:1). Every star in the sky is pointing people to God so they can know Him more.

In addition, God has revealed Himself in Providence. What do I mean by that? I mean that everybody's heart tells them that there's something beyond them. Something out there seems to be controlling and orchestrating this thing that we call life. Call it Providence. It means that God is involved in the world that we live in. Providence tugs upon the human heart to keep looking for a God whom it might not even know yet.

In fact, I believe that God has inscribed eternity upon every heart. A number of years ago, a missionary wrote a book entitled *Eternity in Their Hearts.* Everywhere he would travel in the world, he would tell the story of God the Father sending Jesus, His Son, to the earth to die for the sins of humanity and then how He was raised and sits at the heavenly Father's right hand, and how Jesus sent the Holy Spirit to earth to help people. This missionary reported that every time he would tell the story, without exception and in every culture, his listeners would say, "Oh yeah, we know who He is." They wouldn't necessarily call Him by the name of Jesus. but they would show him something that honored the Son of God. For instance, they would show him a totem pole with an inscription that represented God the Father, and then another set of inscriptions that represented His Son and the Spirit of that God. This missionary wrote that God seems to have inscribed eternity in the human heart. (Not that this means all people are saved. No one can be saved unless they have given their lives to Jesus.) I think we can agree that everyone knows there's something bigger out there, even if we don't know His name. Sometimes we call it the God-sized hole in the human heart.

God has also revealed Himself in the commentaries of history. In every culture we can see how God's hand has been working in the affairs of human history orchestrating a progressive direction for civilization. Of course, God reveals Himself through the pages of His Divine Word.

When you open it, the words jump off the pages and they tell you about God. He remains unknowable; but even so, He reveals Himself in particular through His Son, Jesus Christ, who said, "Whoever has seen me has seen the Father" (John 14:9 NRSV).

HIS WAYS ARE FAR ABOVE OUR WAYS

So we find ourselves in a contradictory position: we seek a God who wants to make Himself known to us; and, yet, He is One who will always remain unknowable—too big for us to understand. So many things will always remain beyond our full comprehension.

Take the Trinity, for example: God the Father, God the Son, and God the Holy Spirit who are three distinct Persons, yet one. We are familiar with the attempts to explain this. "Well, He's like water, which can be a liquid, a frozen solid, and a vapor. Its three distinct forms." Or, "He's like an egg, with the shell, the white and the yoke. All three of them make up one egg." These are just fallible human attempts to understand an eternal God who cannot be explained.

Here is another example of how God exceeds our comprehension. The book of Ezekiel portrays Him as having four faces—the face of a lion, the face of a man, the face of an ox, and the face of an eagle—and each face represents a different part of His nature. There's more. With four faces, one on each side, God has no back! This shows us why you cannot back God into a corner, and why regardless of which direction you go, He's always going forward. God is so vast that you and I will spend an eternity discovering His limitlessness, and we will never have to look over the same part of Him twice. Even in Heaven, every time we will look at Him, we will notice a different facet of His grace.

JOB USED TO THINK HE KNEW GOD

At the root, I believe this was Job's conflict. He was a godly man, and he thought he understood God; but when God allowed Job's life to fall apart, Job found out that he didn't know his God after all. His circumstances didn't seem to be lining up within the parameters of his theological understanding of God. He found himself in a monumental conflict. It's a good thing that God put the book of Job in the Bible so we could learn an important perspective.

Just for a quick review: the first attack came against his family, and we read about it in chapter one. A tornado knocked down the house, killing all of his young adult children who were inside. When he heard the devastating news, Job stood firm in his faith. Then in chapter two, Job was stricken with painful boils from the top of his head to the bottom of his feet. All he could do was sit in one place, scraping at his skin with a potsherd, a piece of broken pottery. His suffering was almost impossible to watch. As a result, his wife began to crack. She told him, "Job, curse God so He'll kill you, and you can die" (see Job 2:9). The Bible says that in all of this, Job didn't sin. In fact, Job observed that we humans seem to be better able to accept good from God than bad. We want to be blessed, but we don't want to have trouble. (This sounds like many Christians I know.)

Along came Job's three friends, Bildad, Eliphaz, and Zophar. Having heard about Job's trouble, they came to his house. When they saw him, they were so appalled that they sat down for seven days without speaking a word to him. This situation was beyond words. How could such a righteous man be forced to suffer such great torment?

By chapter three, Job was beginning to crack. He cursed the day he was born. I find this strangely encouraging, because I'm much like that myself. The first time an attack comes, I rebuke the devil, square my shoulders, and praise God. I get the victory. Then another attack comes but the first attack hasn't left yet. I'm still saying, "Praise God," except now I'm not dancing while I do it. I'm just kind of muttering, "Praise God, I've got the victory; I'm just holding on. Hallelujah!" Then when that attack doesn't leave either, I begin to consider throwing in the towel. This is where we can start to learn some important lessons from Job.

Lesson Number One: Your trials are always personal.

The devil knows how to push your buttons. The devil knows exactly where to hit you to get you to break. He knew how to test Job where it hurt the most. He doesn't afflict people in the same ways. He might hit you in the area of finances. For me, he might confine his attack to the area of sickness. He knows exactly how to make your trial personal.

God had said, "Man, look at My servant Job." The devil had said, "Yeah, but I know exactly how to get to him. Take Your hand of blessing off him and let me deprive him of what he has and then he'll curse You."

Well, he didn't. God took His hand of protection off Job. He lost everything that he held dear, but he kept his faith. Then the devil took his health. God said, "You can touch him but you can't kill him." (The devil is always on a leash. He can go only so far. God will always pull him back before he's crossed the line.) Under that assault, Job became weak. For the next thirty-three chapters, his friends Bildad, Eliphaz, and Zophar were trying to figure out Job's problem. "What in the world did you do wrong, Buddy, to deserve what's going on in your life?" Now that's the kind of friends you need around you when you're in trouble, right? For thirty-three chapters!

Lesson Number Two: The length of the trial always determines your weariness.

Anybody can hold on to their faith when they're attacked once. Anybody can hold on to their faith when they're attacked twice, but what happens when your prayers are not answered and when the attacks don't leave for thirty days and sixty days and ninety days, or maybe a year, or maybe two years? You're still going to the altar. You're still paying your tithe. You're still giving sacrifices to God; but, somehow, nothing is changing. Your weariness grows. You try to figure out why this is happening, but neither you nor your friends have any idea what to do.

Lesson Number Three: When you're in the night, be careful about people's advice.

Many times it's better to go through your mess with nobody but yourself and Jesus than to bring in a Bildad, Eliphaz, or a Zophar who will give you bad advice and keep you in your mess. Maybe the reason Job had to endure from chapter three all the way to chapter thirty-two before anything started to change for him was that he was listening to his three friends. All of us must go through night seasons when we don't know what God is doing. In a night season of your life, you need to be careful about the people you let come into your inner circle to give you advice. If someone gives you the wrong advice, they could keep you in your trouble even longer.

Lesson Number Four: God does not give us songs in the day. He gives songs in the night.

Late in the book of Job, a fourth character comes into the story. His name is Elihu. The Bible says he's a young man. First, he listens to the others. Then, irritated with the way things are going, he speaks up and begins to tell Job what his mistake was. He says, "You're accusing God of being unjust. Job, you're so mixed up. You keep asking God why He is doing this to you. Why? Why? Why? I want to give you a revelation. That's the wrong question. You will never, ever figure it out. Instead of asking, 'Why is this happening?' You should be asking 'Where is the God who gives me a victory song in the middle of my night season?'" (Now some people think that Elihu was misled and that the information that he gave to Job was wrong. I don't think so, because God never rebuked Elihu when He rebuked Job's other friends.)

GOD BREAKS THROUGH THE DARKNESS

God broke through for Job, because He will always come on behalf of each of His children. Time after time, the Bible shows God breaking through darkness and confusion. For example, look at the creation event itself:

> *In the beginning God created the heaven and the earth. And the earth was without form, and void; and darkness was upon the face of the deep. And the Spirit of God moved upon the face of the waters. And God said, Let there be light: and there was light* (Genesis 1:1-3 KJV).

God Himself , who is light, stepped into the darkness and said, "Let there be light," which put a dividing line between darkness and light so that He could call the darkness *night* and the light *day*, because the sun, moon, and stars did not showup until the third day. When darkness is covering everything, when chaos rules, when the world is in trouble and when nobody can help it—not the scientists, the politicians, or the theologians—at the darkest-seeming moment, that's when God breaks in.

God broke through the darkness for Abraham. God promised him, "You're going to have a son." For twenty-five years, he stood on that promise; yet, he had no son, It was a dark time. Sodom and Gomorrah were slated for destruction. Sarah and Abraham grew too old to have children. Then one day, the angel of the Lord brought God's power into their lives, Sarah conceived, and nine months later she bore the child Isaac who had been promised so long before. God's light came in the darkest time.

Later in the book of Exodus we read about the children of Israel in Egyptian captivity. When the plague of darkness covered the land in Egypt, light shone for the Israelites in Goshen (see Exodus 10:23). God's light kept shining in the midst of the dreadful darkness.

In addition, think about the birth of Jesus. The nation of Israel was suffering under Roman rule. For four hundred years, no prophetic revelation had pierced the darkness. In the midst of that endless night, light came to some shepherd boys were camped in a field.

And behold, an angel of the Lord stood before them, and the glory of the Lord shone around them, and they were greatly afraid. ...And suddenly there was with the angel a multitude of the heavenly host praising God and saying: "Glory to God in the highest, and on earth peace, goodwill toward men!" (Luke 2:9,13-14)

In the midst of the darkness of the night, God broke in and changed their lives with a song. Humanity had been lost for thousands of years because of the sin of Adam and Eve, but now the light of the world had come, piercing the darkness with news of a babe wrapped in swaddling clothes. That baby was Jesus, the Word of God and the Light of the world. Here's how John described Him:

In the beginning was the Word, and the Word was with God, and the Word was God. He was in the beginning with God. All things came into being through him, and without him not one thing came into being. What has come into being in him was life, and the life was the light of all people. The light shines in the darkness, and the darkness did not overcome it (John 1:1-5 NRSV).

In other words, whenever God decides to step into your personal dark time, the darkness cannot overcome it.

So instead of asking God "Why," start asking, "Where is the God I know?" Confess the truth that even in the midst of pain and misery you serve the God who always shows up. His light turns your life around, puts a song in your heart and a spring in your step.

GOD COMES THROUGH

Think of Paul and Silas. They had been badly beaten. They were in pain and in trouble, but in the darkness of that hour God gave them a song—the sound of that song in the middle of the night broke their chains. Shackles fell to the ground (see Acts 16). They didn't wait until morning to worship God. They sang to God in the darkest night, and He turned their darkness into day. God is the master of turning darkness into light! In fact, I'm convinced that's the reason He told Israel to count their days starting from the evening—evening and the morning for one day (see Genesis 1:5).

We might not even see Him come through because it's going to be dark, but one thing we can be sure of—although tonight might bring some weeping mixed with our worship, tomorrow morning there'll be joy. We praise Him until we get a release. It's more than singing a chorus and clapping our hands together. We start looking for Him. We just forget about the unresolved conflict of *why* and start looking for the God who shows up in the night. We won't ever be able to resolve everything. We won't know some things until we get to Heaven. What we need more than answers is to have God step into our current night.

A believer's praise is a powerful weapon. When the devil hears it, it disarms him. Praise does not make logical sense. Praise says, "Even though it looks bad, God is still God, and He comes through in the night." Praise really confuses the spirit realm. The devil doesn't like it at all.

God came through for Job, and the devil gave up the fight. As soon as Elihu finished talking, Job prayed for his friends. He said, "Lord, forgive my foolish friends." He quit asking God why. He could see that nobody could give him an answer. He could see that the issue isn't *why*. The issue is, "Where's God?" Where is the God who gives victory songs in the night? As soon as Job got this revelation, he got double for his trouble:

> ...*The Lord gave Job twice as much as he had owned before.*
> ...*The Lord blessed the last part of Job's life even more than*
> *the first part. Job had fourteen thousand sheep, six thousand*
> *camels, a thousand teams of oxen, and a thousand female*

*donkeys. Job also had seven sons and three daughters. ...
There were no other women in all the land as beautiful as
Job's daughters. And their father Job gave them land to own
along with their brothers. After this, Job lived one hundred
forty years. He lived to see his children, grandchildren,
great-grandchildren, and great-great-grandchildren* (Job
42:10,12-13,15-16 NCV).

The same thing applies to every one of us. It doesn't matter what
kind of trouble you're in, or even if you have created your own trouble.
God wants to come through for you. Before anything else you have to
accept Jesus as Savior and Lord of your life. Then you will have something to sing about. Nothing is going to turn around in your life until
you have Jesus; but after you have Him, God will start something brand
new with you. Songs in the night can become a wonderful part of your
new life.

Chapter 6

A NOISE OF WAR IN THE CAMP

When Joshua heard the noise of the people as
they shouted, he said to Moses, "There is a
noise of war in the camp" (EXODUS 32:17).

When Moses went up on Mount Sinai for an extended period of
time, God gave him detailed instructions about how to set up the tabernacle. Down in the valley, the people of Israel, under the leadership
of Aaron, decided to fashion a golden calf, which they began to worship. Angered by their idol worship, God commanded Moses to go down
the mountain. Halfway down, Moses found Joshua waiting for him—he
was standing there listening to people in the valley below. When Moses
descended to the spot where Joshua was waiting, Joshua made a statement that every believer should take note of. He said, "There's a noise of
war in the camp."

And Moses turned and went down from the mountain, and the two tablets of the Testimony were in his hand. The tablets were written on both sides; on the one side and on the other they were written. Now the tablets were the work of God, and the writing was the writing of God engraved on the tablets. And when Joshua heard the noise of the people as they shouted, he said to Moses, "There is a noise of war in the camp." But he [Moses] said: "It is not the noise of the shout of victory, nor the noise of the cry of defeat, but the sound of singing I hear" (Exodus 32:15-18).

The people in the valley were worshipping an idol. What did their worship entail? We can get some clues from the nuances of meaning of the word *worship* itself. The Hebrew word for worship is *shachah,* and it means to bow down or prostrate oneself. Apparently while in Egypt, they had learned to worship an agricultural deity in the form of a golden calf. The ancient Egyptians would worship it by bowing down before it and by even kissing it on the mouth. (The Septuagint, the Greek translation of the Hebrew Bible, uses a Greek word, *proskuneo,* which clearly conveys the idea of kissing the statue. It meant to kiss like a dog licking a man's hand.) That may have been what was happening down in the valley in front of the golden calf; the people may have been bowing down in reverence before it and even kissing it, possibly on its mouth. As they took turns giving worship to the golden calf, they were celebrating fervently.

Moses could tell that they were not worshipping God. He exclaimed, "It is not the noise of the shout of victory, nor the noise of the cry of defeat, but the sound of singing I hear" (Exodus 32:18). Their clamor expressed no love for God. Paul described such an outcry as "sounding brass or a clanging cymbal" (1 Corinthians 13:1).

It makes me wonder—what does the great God of Heaven think when He listens to our worship services? Much of the time, sadly, He hears only a group of people who are making worship-like sounds while going through the motions. True worshippers will be expressing their heartfelt adoration toward Him. They probably understand the spiritual dynamics of worship, unlike the people who perform the act of worship but who lack a heart of worship. (How many times have you gone to church and walked through the motions with your heart never engaging Heaven?)

WORSHIP IS WARFARE

Moses and Joshua could hear the sounds of the celebration coming up from the camp—music, dancing, and shouting—and yet Joshua referred to it as the noise of war. In their case, the people were about to be corrected severely for following Aaron when he set up the golden calf. Their idolatrous worship was called "the noise of war" because even faulty worship sets off unseen conflicts. If that is the case, just think what true, heartfelt worship can do! Seize this spiritual principle, and your life will never be the same. I believe the reason people do not see the value in being true worshippers is that they do not know the power of praise and worship. Worship is one of the believer's most powerful weapons in the spiritual warfare that occurs out of the sight of our earthbound eyes.

We can see a clear example of worship as a heavenly weapon in the victory song of Deborah and Barak after their successful campaign against Sisera. They sang, "The stars fought from heaven, from their courses they fought against Sisera" (Judges 5:20 NRSV). According to the order and direction of the Lord of hosts, the stars somehow fought against Sisera, either by using malignant influences or by causing storms of hail and thunder. In some unique way, the heavenly bodies—although not arrested as when the sun stood still at Joshua's word, but by continuing on in their courses—fought against Sisera. The whole of creation is at war with those who oppose the God of Heaven. Even the river of Kishon was released to sweep away multitudes of the enemy soldiers (see Judges 5:21). Heaven and earth fought together to rout the enemies of God's people. Then a song of worship and thanksgiving burst forth from the lips of Deborah and Barak, a song that has been sung ever since. We still have the words. Worship *is* warfare!

Throughout the Old Testament, we can see a pattern in war strategy: putting worshippers in front of armies as they go into battle. When the Moabites, Ammonites, and Edomites invaded Judah, Jehoshaphat, the king, faced the battle of his life. As a result he sought the Lord's will through prayer. God responded to him through Jahaziel, "Don't be afraid of this multitude. The battle is not yours but Mine. You won't need to fight, but you will see the victory" (see 2 Chronicles 20:15-17). Upon hearing this assurance, the Levites praised the Lord "with a loud voice on high" (2 Chronicles 20:19 KJV). How would the people of Judah be able to win this war without fighting? In a highly unusual tactic, Jehoshaphat put the choir out in front of the army (see 2 Chronicles 20:21). The choir began to praise the Lord in anticipation of the truth of the prophetic word. As they did so, the enemy was defeated (v. 22). Here's how it went:

> *When he had taken counsel with the people, he appointed those who were to sing to the Lord and praise him in holy splendor, as they went before the army, saying, "Give thanks to the Lord, for his steadfast love endures forever." As they began to sing and praise, the Lord set an ambush against the Ammonites, Moab, and Mount Seir, who had come against Judah, so that they were routed. For the Ammonites and Moab attacked the inhabitants of Mount Seir, destroying them utterly; and when they had made an end of the inhabitants of Seir, they all helped to destroy one another. When Judah came to the watchtower of the wilderness, they looked toward the multitude; they were corpses lying on the ground; no one had escaped* (2 Chronicles 20:21-24 NRSV).

The praise of Jehoshaphat's choir (unlike much of our praise and worship today) had a triumphant ring of victory: "Let the high praises of God be in their mouth, and a two-edged sword in their hand" (Psalm 149:6 KJV). Jehoshaphat and his choir went out to praise God, and thereby they won the victory. Armed only with instruments and their singing, they changed the outcome. The battle was won through the weapon of worship. I believe that this principle applies to any battle or war faced by anyone who knows God. Warfare can be won by the weapon of worship alone!

ANGELS ATTENDING

The spiritual warfare that seems to get stirred up by worship proves that angels (both good ones and fallen angels—demons) are present behind the scenes. This helps explain the succinct statement in First Corinthians 11:10 (RSV), in which Paul advised, "That [woman being created after man] a woman ought to have a veil on her head, because of the angels." (In his letter to the Corinthians, Paul was counseling the church within the context of corporate worship, indicating in various ways that we should be careful how we approach worship.)

According to Hebrews 1:14, angels are "ministering spirits sent forth to minister for them who shall be heirs of salvation." In other words, angels have been working on behalf of believers up to the present day. They were especially involved in the ministry of Jesus and in the New Testament church. I have no doubt that angels are still very active in the lives of believers and in God's church today, and that fallen angels are also prowling around "like a roaring lion, seeking someone to devour" (1 Peter 5:8 RSV). Wherever possible, fallen angels try to thwart the will of God in our lives. (For a glimpse of their doing this behind the scenes, see Daniel 10:12-13.)

Did you realize that angels, both fallen and good, are attending your worship services? I believe that when we gather for corporate worship or start to worship privately, a sound of warfare gets released in the heavens. Angels assemble in response to the sound, and by the direction of the Holy Spirit they do business in our lives. Sometimes that business involves warfare with the evil spirits who may also be present in the place.

In one of our services at the church where I am pastor, we had a powerful outpouring of God's presence during an intense time of prophetically charged worship. The atmosphere was electric with the glory of God. Believers could physically feel the His power. Suddenly a young man who was totally blind received his sight; this event was witnessed by almost a thousand people. Along with the rest of the congregation, I was filled with awe as we watched this young man (whom we all knew well) see for the first time. His precious young wife wept as she watched her husband read signs, count fingers, and point out colors. What a miracle! Imagine the joyful excitement of the congregation!

I believe that the healing occurred because we had entered into such a time of genuine and intense corporate worship. The night before that service, something strange had happened. I had awakened out of a deep sleep, sat up, and heard these words, "Angels will be at church tomorrow!" I jumped out of the bed and immediately went into a time of prayer, seeking God's direction for the next day's worship. I felt drawn to the story of Joshua and the walls of Jericho. I began to read that story in my Bible carefully and repeatedly. That's when I noticed something that I had never seen before: when Joshua arrived at the walls of the city, the angel of the Lord was already there. All of a sudden out of my spirit came rushing these words, "Angels will be at church tomorrow! Tell the people all they have to do is show up with a shout!"

Then when the presence and power of God became tangible in the service the next day, I stood and declared to the people what I felt the Lord had said. Immediately the place erupted with a roar that sounded like a thousand lions, and more miracles started happening all over the building. Do you see what I mean when I say that when we worship, a sound gets released in the heavens and the angels respond to it. All we have to do is show up and be ready to shout!

Here is something else to ponder. what if angels are not the only heavenly beings you can expect at your worship services? What if Jesus Himself were to attend? In the following chapters, I am going to prove to you that He does. I will then show you what He does when He gets there.

Remember, the sound of worship summons angels and, therefore, often arouses warfare in the heavenly realm. Don't forget that the Lord is looking for worshippers, not just noise that sounds like worship.

Chapter 7

JESUS SINGS AND GOD DANCES

The Lord thy God in the midst of thee is mighty;
he will save, he will rejoice over thee with joy;
he will rest in his love, he will joy over thee
with singing (ZEPHANIAH 3:17 KJV)

Worship is a spiritual affair. Jesus said, "God is a Spirit: and they that worship him must worship him in spirit and in truth" (John 4:24 KJV). You can't truly worship God without engaging your spirit with His Spirit.

The key word in this verse is *must*. Jesus is not merely making a suggestion. Rather, He is insisting that this worshipping "in spirit and in truth" is *essential*—it's the only way to approach God. That's why Paul worded this statement as he did: "For God is my witness, whom I serve with my spirit in the gospel of his Son..." (Romans 1:9 RSV).

The context of this statement in John 4 is a discussion on the subject of life-giving water; therefore, we can say that true spiritual worship is closely connected to God's personalized life-giving activity. When you offer your spirit to Him in praise and worship, His Spirit enlivens your spirit. New life flows into you from the Creator. It's too good to miss, but yet many believers do.

Genuine worship occurs only when the spirit, the immortal and invisible part of man, speaks to and meets with God. It is the spirit of a man, through worship, which attains to friendship and intimacy with God. We must understand the spiritual dynamics of true Spirit-led worship because all other worship activities are nothing more than religious calisthenics.

Because true worship is essentially spiritual, we must take a deep look at the realm of the Spirit. What really transpires during our worship? Two verses in the second chapter of Hebrews provide a fascinating glimpse of what is happening in a worship service:

> *For the one who sanctifies and those who are sanctified all have one Father. For this reason Jesus is not ashamed to call them brothers and sisters, saying, "I will proclaim your name to my brothers and sisters, in the midst of the congregation I will praise you"* (Hebrews 2:11-12 NRSV).

This passage reveals the powerful position of believers, and Jesus' attitude toward them. Think of it—He is not ashamed to call us His brothers and sisters! He considers Himself to be one with believers because we all have the same Father. We are brothers and sisters with Jesus Christ. He says we "all have one Father." Paul restates this truth in his letter to the Romans: "...and if children, then heirs, heirs of God and joint heirs with Christ..." (Romans 8:17 NRSV). Whatever the Father God will do for His Son Jesus, He will do for us. Hallelujah!

LOOK WHO'S TALKING!

We are joint heirs with Jesus, His brothers and sisters. What does our Lord and brother Jesus do in one of our worship services? Hebrews

2:12 explains. ("I will proclaim your name to my brothers and sisters, in the midst of the congregation I will praise you.")

Did you know that Jesus attends church? He does, as we can learn from a number of other Scriptures. For example:

> *For where two or three are gathered in my name, there am I in the midst of them* (Matthew 18:20 RSV).

> *You sit as the Holy One. The praises of Israel are your throne* (Psalm 22:3 NCV).

Simply put, when believers come together in a worship setting, spiritual activity starts occurring. According to Hebrews 2:12, when Jesus comes into a worship service, He begins to do at least two things. He declares the names of God to His brethren and even joins the congregation in singing worship to the Father. Let's take a look at what that means.

"I will proclaim your name to my brothers and sisters...." Note that Jesus is the one doing the speaking. God revealed His name to Moses as *Yahweh*: "God said to Moses, 'I AM WHO I AM.' ...this is my name for ever, and thus I am to be remembered throughout all generations" (Exodus 3:14-15 RSV). Until that time the children of Israel, including Abraham, Isaac, and Jacob, had not known God as Jehovah, but rather by the name of God Almighty (see Exodus 6:3). But through Moses, God began to reveal to His people the full meaning of His redemptive name. *Jehovah* means "the self-existent one or eternal one who reveals Himself." The Lord instructed Moses that Jehovah is His name forever. Using this name would remind Israel of His covenant with them, His word of promises is everlasting because He Himself is eternal and unchangeable in His nature. He is, therefore, faithful and unchangeable in His Word and promises.

However, as different needs arose among the children of Israel during their history, the Lord revealed Himself more specifically as the one who could faithfully meet those needs. There is only one God Jehovah; but He has a plethora of attributes. He wants His people to know that He is not an inaccessible Supreme Being suspended in a place called Heaven. In all of His sovereignty, He wants to be intimately involved in the lives of His people. The redemptive names of God reveal His redemptive relationship to believers.

HE MEETS EVERY NEED

In the Old Testament, we can find seven redemptive names of the Lord that demonstrate how capable He is in meeting every area of human need:

- Jehovah Jireh—The Lord our Provision
- Jehovah Rapha—The Lord our Healer
- Jehovah Nissi—The Lord our Banner
- Jehovah Shalom—The Lord our Peace
- Jehovah Rohi—The Lord our Shepherd
- Jehovah Tsidkenu—The Lord our Righteousness
- Jehovah Shammah—The Lord is Here

With those names in mind, let's return to Hebrews 2:12 and the concept of Jesus attending our worship services. When He arrives, He is seeking the true worshippers (see John 4:23). When He finds one, He declares to that person's spirit one of the redemptive names of God. For example, if someone in the service needs financial or material assistance, Jesus makes a point of saying, "I am Jehovah Jireh—your Provider!" Those who need divine healing hear the Spirit of Jesus say, "I am Jehovah Rapha—your Healer!" The single mom in the back of the room whose life has been shattered by divorce and who does not know which way to turn finds Jesus walking up to her and saying, "I am Jehovah Shalom—your Peace."

Have you ever noticed that there are times right in the middle of worship when you can feel a shift or a change in your spirit? Your circumstances might not have changed, but you feel encouraged in spite of contrary issues. In our congregation we have witnessed numerous miracles—blind eyes opened, deaf ears healed, cancerous tumors dissolved, etc. In every instance, the miracles have come during times of heavy worship. I believe that in those times Jesus walks into the room and starts whispering the redemptive names of God to the spiritual ears of individual people, based on their personal needs. He and His Father care for those who have placed their trust in God.

As Jesus is declaring the names of God to the brethren, He gets caught up in worship and begins to sing with the church to the Father. That's what the second part of verse twelve tells us: "in the midst of the congregation I will praise you." In the midst of the worshipping church, Jesus starts singing praises to God the Father along with the congregation. It is one thing for me, a fallible, weak human being, to be worshipping the Father; but it is another thing altogether when Jesus starts singing to the Father alongside me!

THE FATHER REJOICES

In the meantime, what is God the Father doing in Heaven, while Jesus and the angels are active in our church services?

I quoted this passage at the beginning of the chapter: "The Lord thy God in the midst of thee is mighty; he will save, he will rejoice over thee with joy; he will rest in his love, he will joy over thee with singing" (Zephaniah 3:17 KJV). This passage is loaded with revelation about heavenly activity. God in our midst is mighty. Our worship is what attracts Him into our midst: "You sit as the Holy One. The praises of Israel are your throne" (Psalm 22:3 NCV). As He inhabits our praise, God rejoices over us with joy and singing. If you look up the word *rejoice* in a dictionary, you find that it means "to be joyful, happy, delighted, elated, ecstatic, overjoyed, jubilant, rapturous; to jump for joy, to be on cloud nine, to be in seventh heaven; to celebrate, or to cheer."

Get this picture in your mind: God, cheering and jumping in the heavens, filled with joy and happiness concerning a group of people who are worshipping Him (accompanied by His Son and many angels). The word *joy* here can mean "to twirl and dance with great and happy emotion"; as worshippers sing to God, He is dancing in the heavens and singing back!

TOGETHER IN WORSHIP

When we tie all of this together, we get a wonderful picture of what is happening in the spirit realm during worship. Angels come into the service for ministry purposes. Jesus, enthroned upon our praises, begins to walk in the midst of the congregation declaring the names of God to the ones who are truly worshipping, His brothers and sisters. At some point, Jesus joins in with the church, singing praises unto the Father. In Heaven, God the Father rises from His throne, rejoicing and dancing over us, His children, as He sings a love song back to us. What a dynamic picture!

When I was growing up, I was always taught that Jesus and God frown on dancing, but I have since learned that they are not nearly as religious as some believers are. In fact, because Jesus is the express image of the Father, He rejoices just as much as His Father does. We can find clear evidence of this in Scripture.

In Luke 10 Jesus commissioned His disciples for ministry and sent them out in His power. When they returned, they were all rejoicing over the powerful manifestations that they had experienced. Then Jesus "rejoiced in spirit" (Luke 10:21 KJV). I used to think, as do most Christians, that when a sinner gets saved, all of the angels rejoice in Heaven; that is how we learn it in church. This is not quite the whole picture, however. Look what the Word actually says: "Likewise, I say unto you, there is joy in the presence of the angels of God over one sinner that repenteth" (Luke 15:10 KJV). Notice that it does not say the angels rejoice; it says that there is joy *in the presence of* the angels. I believe that God and Jesus are celebrating in the heavens and that their joy is contagious! Also, I think that this gives all the more reason to offer thanks in joyful worship at every opportunity.

Chapter 8

SATAN KNOWS THE POWER OF WORSHIP

*You were the anointed cherub who covers; I
established you; you were on the holy mountain
of God; you walked back and forth in the midst
of fiery stones. You were perfect in your ways
from the day you were created, till iniquity
was found in you* (EZEKIEL 28:14-15).

Scripture carries layers and layers of revelation about the Kingdom of God. Just when we think we have understood everything, God's Spirit shows us something new. Paul calls this the "manifold wisdom of God" (Ephesians 3:10). We will spend eternity discovering the limitless shining facets of His glory.

Woven into the fabric of Ezekiel 28 is one of those unexpected revelations. The chapter is a curious one because its verses, while apparently describing the same individual, a sovereign ruler of the city of Tyre (in modern-day southern Lebanon, just north of Israel), the "prince of Tyre" (addressed in verses 1-10) seems in fact to be quite distinct from the "king of Tyre" (addressed in verses 11-19).

These two rulers received two different declarations from God through the prophet Ezekiel. The first was of judgment, and the second was of lamentation. It is very evident that both of these individuals were guilty of the sin of pride. Both possessed great wisdom and wealth; however, they abused their privileges and, thus, offended the God of Heaven. Many theologians believe that the prince of Tyre mentioned in verses 1-10 was a ruler of the city of Tyre when Nebuchadnezzar invaded in about 573 B.C.; but they view the king of Tyre (in verses 11-19) as Satan, the enemy of God and of the Jewish people. They base their interpretation, in part, on the fact that the prince is called "a man" in verse two, but the king is called the "anointed cherub" in verse fourteen. The use of the word *cherub* shows that this king is an angelic creature. A cherub is a powerful angel (not a chubby baby angel, as is often portrayed on old-fashioned valentines). Another clue to the subject of these verses is found in verse 14, which relates that this angelic creature was once found in the Garden of Eden and in the holy mountain of God.

Here is the entire passage about the fallen angelic being known for the prophet's purposes as the king of Tyre:

> *Moreover the word of the Lord came to me, saying, "Son of man, take up a lamentation for the king of Tyre, and say to him, 'Thus says the Lord God: You were the seal of perfection, full of wisdom and perfect in beauty. You were in Eden, the garden of God; every precious stone was your covering: The sardius, topaz, and diamond, beryl, onyx, and jasper, sapphire, turquoise, and emerald with gold. The workmanship of your timbrels and pipes was prepared for you on the day you were created. You were the anointed cherub*

who covers; I established you; you were on the holy mountain of God; you walked back and forth in the midst of fiery stones. You were perfect in your ways from the day you were created, till iniquity was found in you. By the abundance of your trading you became filled with violence within, and you sinned; therefore I cast you as a profane thing out of the mountain of God; and I destroyed you, O covering cherub, from the midst of the fiery stones. Your heart was lifted up because of your beauty; you corrupted your wisdom for the sake of your splendor; I cast you to the ground, I laid you before kings, that they might gaze at you. You defiled your sanctuaries by the multitude of your iniquities, by the iniquity of your trading; therefore I brought fire from your midst; it devoured you, and I turned you to ashes upon the earth in the sight of all who saw you. All who knew you among the peoples are astonished at you; you have become a horror, and shall be no more forever'" (Ezekiel 28:11-19).

In interpreting this passage, people often refer to Isaiah 14:12 for its portrayal of the heavenly rebellion and fall of a powerful angel:

How you are fallen from heaven, O Lucifer, son of the morning! How you are cut down to the ground, you who weakened the nations!

I believe that the king of Tyre, Satan, must have energized the earthly ruler known as the prince of Tyre, using him to accomplish Satan's own evil purposes. This also occurred elsewhere in the scriptural accounts, such as in the book of Daniel and in the Revelation of John, where the Antichrist, who is an earthly ruler, is energized by Satan to accomplish his wicked agenda during the end-times tribulation. Other places in the Bible tell how Satan tries to control the leaders of nations. One, in First Chronicles 21, deals with Satan as he inspired David to take a census, after which David repented. Later, there is the account of Satan's temptation of Jesus in the wilderness. In the latter example, Satan clearly "tips his hand" regarding his agenda of maintaining earthly control:

> *Then the devil led Jesus to the top of a very high mountain and showed him all the kingdoms of the world and all their splendor. The devil said, "If you will bow down and worship me, I will give you all these things." Jesus said to the devil, "Go away from me, Satan! It is written in the Scriptures, 'You must worship the Lord your God and serve only him'"* (Matthew 4:8-10 NCV).

SATAN'S ORIGINAL ROLE

Satan, also known as Lucifer, began as an obedient angel, but he rebelled against God and led an attempt to steal God's throne. Before he rebelled, his coverings were jewel-studded and glorious to behold: "Every precious stone was your covering: the sardius, topaz, and diamond, beryl, onyx, and jasper, sapphire, turquoise, and emerald with gold" (Ezekiel 28:13). These are the same jewels found on the breastplate of the high priest of the people of Israel (see Exodus 28:17-20), which speaks of Lucifer's special priestly authority.

According to Ezekiel 28:13 and Isaiah 14:11, the angel Lucifer also had special musical abilities. Various translations mention a range of instruments—timbrels, pipes, viols, harps, lyres, and stringed instruments. In essence, Lucifer functioned as a heavenly worship leader. (With all of the world's perverted music and lyrics, one must wonder if Satan is still playing music in his rebellious state. Could the world's music be emulating the wicked sound from the fallen angel?)

The next verse is the one about the anointed cherub, and it goes on to provide an important clue as to the identity and function of this powerful personage: "You were the anointed cherub who covers; I established you; you were on the holy mountain of God; you walked back and forth in the midst of fiery stones. You were perfect in your ways from the day you were created…" (Ezekiel 28:14-15). The clause "who covers" indicates a heavenly being with a specific assignment of authority over something. The question becomes "What does he control?" The answer is found in several passages. To find the answer, we can refer back to the same two verses of Ezekiel, where we read that he was in the Garden of Eden and also upon the holy mountain of God, neither of which means Heaven. It seems that Isaiah 14:12 confirms the conclusion that he was positioned on earth and that he had authority over the earth.

The next few verses provide more of the story about Satan's rebellion and fall from authority:

> *You said in your heart, "I will ascend to heaven; above the stars of God. I will set my throne on high; I will sit on the mount of assembly in the far north; I will ascend above the heights of the clouds, I will make myself like the Most High."* *But you are brought down to Sheol, to the depths of the Pit* (Isaiah 14:13-15 RSV).

If Lucifer were already in Heaven, why would he need to *ascend* to get *above the heights of the clouds*? The clouds are part of earth's atmosphere. The implication is that Satan was an angel who was assigned at one time authority over the earth. Evidently, he tried to lead a rebellion to overthrow God, and a large contingent of the angels joined him in the mutiny. Here is how his fall is pictured in the book of Revelation: "The great dragon was thrown down, that ancient serpent, who is called the Devil and Satan, the deceiver of the whole world—he was thrown down to the earth, and his angels were thrown down with him" (Revelation 12:9 NRSV).

WHAT SATAN KNOWS ABOUT WORSHIP

So we see that Lucifer was no ordinary angel. He was an angelic creature of unusual beauty with a powerful gift for leading worship. He was persuasive; many lesser angels followed him. He *covered the earth* in his authority—before his rebellion.

Now we can see why Satan fights the worship of believers as he does! With his history of a firsthand experience of the effect of worship upon God and the angels, but also with his fury at losing his position of authority over the earth because of his great rebellion, he was further enraged at God's reassignment of dominion over the earth to the human race He had created. For all intents and purposes, human beings—the ones who are believers—have become Satan's replacement. When people were newly created, they were given dominion over the earth (see Genesis 1:28). That dominion was lost almost immediately through their rebellion, then regained by the sacrifice of the Son of God Jesus Christ. Now, through their vocal chords, hands, fingers, and feet, human believers represent the Father on earth, and they have the ability to produce music and express worship to Him.

Do you see why the enemy interferes with the affairs of nations, sets people against each other, and instigates conflicts even within the Church, and why he tries to interfere with true worship wherever possible? Satan's former authority was associated with his worship abilities; so, no wonder he tries to corrupt true worship in any way possible.

No wonder, also, that one of our greatest warfare tools is the weapon of worship. Nothing moves the heavens like worship! Satan knows this without a doubt because he has seen the effect of worship upon the heavens and the Godhead. He does not want the Body of Christ to discover something so powerful about worship.

To pervert worship, Satan constantly attempts to draw men away from *true worship* to false worship, the worship of idols and other gods. Because human beings were created to worship, people will always worship *something!* It might be beauty or wealth or some definition of success, a husband or a wife or other special person, or the traditions of an institution. People can't help worshipping something because worship was built into them from the very beginning.

Satan fights day and night to keep people from discovering the power of worship because he knows that true worship is the pathway to God-ordained dominion for the Christian Church and its individual members.

Now that we are aware of Satan's strategies we can better resist his ploys with true worship, one of our strongest weapons in triumphing over him.

Chapter 9

BETRAYED BY A KISS

*And while he yet spake, lo, Judas, one of the twelve,
came, and with him a great multitude with swords
and staves, from the chief priests and elders of the
people. Now he that betrayed him gave them a
sign, saying, Whomsoever I shall kiss, that same
is he: hold him fast. And forthwith he came to
Jesus, and said, Hail, master; and kissed him.
And Jesus said unto him, Friend, wherefore art
thou come? Then came they, and laid hands on
Jesus, and took him (Matthew 26:47-50 KJV).*

In Chapter 6, I introduced the Hebrew word for worship, *shachah*,
which means "to bow down or prostrate oneself." In association with
the story of the worship of the golden calf, I also presented the word
proskuneo, which is used in the Septuagint (the Greek translation of the
Hebrew Bible), and which means "to kiss like a dog licking a man's

hand." It has been surmised that Aaron had erected the golden calf and the Israelites were worshipping it in this manner, by bowing down and possibly kissing it on the mouth, because they had learned it in Egypt, as it is known that ancient Egyptians worshipped an agricultural deity in this way.

Needless to say, a kiss is a very intimate, personal action. It can be entirely positive or an expression of corrupted motives. This is why, when the disciple Judas betrayed Jesus with a kiss, his action seems much worse than it already was. In appearance, Judas was showing honor to his Lord (as a person might do in worship). In reality, he was handing Him over for death.

Judas, thinking that Jesus would be hard to find and that the disciples who were with Him would put up a fight, had brought a band of soldiers, armed and carrying lanterns, to arrest Him. Judas failed to understand so much about the Lord. The fact is a kiss was not even necessary, because Jesus clearly told the soldiers who He was:

> *So Judas, procuring a band of soldiers and some officers from the chief priests and the Pharisees, went there with lanterns and torches and weapons. Then Jesus, knowing all that was to befall him, came forward and said to them, "Whom do you seek?" They answered him, "Jesus of Nazareth." Jesus said to them, "I am he"* (John 18:3-5 RSV).

Hail, master was a usual compliment among the Jews. Judas pretended to wish the Lord Jesus continued health while he was aiming for His destruction! It makes me think of other stories in the Word about compliments of this kind—Joab, for instance. Joab pretended by a kiss to inquire tenderly after the health of Amasa, but then he thrust him through with his sword (see 2 Samuel 20:9-10). Such insidious kisses are tantamount to false worship, and the rewards are never good.

"JUDAS" = "PRAISE"

The meaning of the name *Judas* is "thanked, admired, praised"—in a word, praise. Another way of thinking of it is that Judas' very name essentially means "worship." Somehow, he chose to use a distinctly worshipful action as a signal for betrayal. His kiss was corrupt, a weapon of destruction. In that day it was customary for disciples to kiss their teacher upon meeting him; their kiss was a sign of respect and honor. However, Judas' kiss of betrayal was a sign of *dis*respect and *dis*honor. To make matters worse, the Greek verb indicates that Judas kissed Jesus repeatedly, not only once, but multiple times. As it turned out, Judas fulfilled the words of Isaiah, which he must have heard Jesus quote: "This people honors me with their lips, but their heart is far from me; in vain do they worship me, teaching as doctrines the precepts of men" (Matthew 15:8-9 RSV).

Earlier, Judas had scorned the worshipful kisses of others. Do you remember how Mary of Bethany lavished her affection and honor upon Jesus?

> *Six days before the Passover Feast, Jesus went to Bethany, where Lazarus lived.* (Lazarus is the man Jesus raised from the dead.) *There they had a dinner for Jesus. Martha served the food, and Lazarus was one of the people eating with Jesus. Mary brought in a pint of very expensive perfume made from pure nard. She poured the perfume on Jesus' feet, and then she wiped his feet with her hair. And the sweet smell from the perfume filled the whole house. Judas Iscariot, one of Jesus' followers who would later turn against him, was there. Judas said, "This perfume was worth an entire year's wages. Why wasn't it sold and the money given to the poor?" But Judas did not really care about the poor; he said this because he was a thief. He was the one who kept the money box, and he often stole from it* (John 12:1-6 NCV).

In an act of pure love and worship on her part, Mary used a large amount of very costly ointment to anoint Jesus' feet. It would have required a year's wages from a common laborer to purchase the ointment. Like King David, Mary had determined not to give the Lord that which cost her nothing (see 2 Samuel 24:24). This act of worship infiltrated the atmosphere of the house with its powerful fragrance and became a story that has been spread around the world (see Matthew 26:13). Yet who opened his mouth to publicly criticize this beautiful act of worship, which the Lord Himself was commending? Judas.

MERCHANDISING THE ANOINTING

While John recorded the earliest utterance by Judas in the New Testament (quoted in John 12), Matthew recorded his final words: "I have sinned by betraying innocent blood" (Matthew 27:4 NRSV). Both passages make it clear that Judas was a thief and was in the habit of stealing money from the common purse, which had been entrusted to him. I find it interesting that the Greek word for bag or box (found in John 12:6) is *glossokomon*, which originally meant a small case in which mouthpieces for wind instruments were kept. For me, this is a profound connection. Usually the only person who would have carried that kind of bag was a musician. Possibly at one time Judas had been a player of wind instruments, and possibly Jesus chose him for his worship ability. As stated before, Judas' name means praise, and here now we see that he was reported to keep the group's money in a musician's "gig bag."

Therefore, you could say that he was merchandising his anointing— giving up the thing he was created to do (praising God) and instead treasuring money, even stealing some of it for his personal use. When we read about Satan's rebellion and fall in the book of Ezekiel (quoted in full in the previous chapter), we see how Satan, too, pridefully merchandised his anointing: "By the multitude of thy merchandise they have filled the midst of thee with violence, and thou hast sinned: therefore I will cast thee as profane out of the mountain of God: and I will destroy thee, O covering cherub, from the midst of the stones of fire" (Ezekiel 28:16 KJV). This anointed cherub whom God created to rule by worship betrayed the Lord by using his gift for his own personal gain.

I am very concerned about the merchandising of preaching and worship in the Body of Christ by those in full-time Christian service. I understand the necessity of budgets and finances for the operating expenses of the ministries of preachers and worship leaders, and I realize that sometimes products should be made available for purchase that strengthen believers' walks with Christ. On the other hand, I believe that it dishonors God for preachers and worshippers to take what they have been created to do and to merchandise it or promote it for sale. Our gifts and talents are not for sale! Yes, the Lord provides for those of us in full-time ministry through our gifts and talents, but if we allow pride and the lust for money to move us to a place of commercializing our anointing we commit the great sin of betrayal!

I am amazed at the groups and preachers who have set prices on their ministries. Recently, our church hosted two internationally known guests. One had a set price, and the other required nothing more than expenses and a love offering by faith. The one who set a price received his required 3,500 dollars; however, the one who came by faith left with over 15,000 dollars. What was the difference? The difference was the anointing of the Holy Ghost upon the second man's ministry! It strikes me as strange that those ministries who require thousands of dollars up front before they will agree to minister will come and preach about a level of faith that they themselves do not have. Sometimes I wonder if some preachers and singers have ever read what the Bible states:

> *He called his twelve followers together and got ready to send them out two by two and gave them authority over evil spirits. This is what Jesus commanded them: "Take nothing*

for your trip except a walking stick. Take no bread, no bag, and no money in your pockets. Wear sandals, but take only the clothes you are wearing. When you enter a house, stay there until you leave that town. If the people in a certain place refuse to welcome you or listen to you, leave that place. Shake its dust off your feet as a warning to them. ...I tell you the truth, on the Judgment Day it will be better for the towns of Sodom and Gomorrah than for the people of that town (Mark 6:7-11; Matthew 10:15 NCV).

If they were not supposed to take money, then it means that they had to trust God to provide for their ministry. It worked; their ministry was highly successful, and they received adequate provision every step of the way.

KISS THE SON

Judas, the musician and praiser, betrayed Jesus with the kiss of worship by honoring Him with his lips and dishonoring Him with his heart. How many times have you and I come to worship services only to go through the motions of worship without really entering in with our hearts? Are we not, on some level, guilty of Judas' sin? Are we honoring God with our words of worship but failing to engage our hearts? Are we expressing heartfelt love for the Lord in our worship? If you have failed in this area, it is not too late to repent and ask the Lord to forgive you for betraying Him with the kisses of worship. Here's a final word on the subject:

> *Kiss the Son, lest He be angry, and you perish in the way, when His wrath is kindled but a little. Blessed are all those who put their trust in Him* (Psalm 2:12).

Chapter 10

THE THRONE ZONE

*Truly, truly, I say to you, he who believes
in me will also do the works that I do; and
greater works than these will he do, because
I go to the Father* (JOHN 14:12 RSV).

The four books of the Bible that we call the Gospels represent only eighty days of Jesus' three-and-a-half-year ministry. Eighty days. None of the Gospel writers could include all of His miracles, because there were too many of them.

Then, at the end of the Gospel of John, we read, "There are many other things Jesus did. If every one of them were written down, I suppose the whole world would not be big enough for all the books that would be written" (John 21:25 NCV). If all of the miracles of Jesus could have been written down, all the libraries in the world could not contain the collections of accounts!

Yet we see so many of His mighty works in the pages of the Gospels—everything from changing water into wine to raising the dead—that we are awed by Him. Jesus is so supernatural.

"Of course," you may say, "He was God's Son. What do you expect?" But you need to know that when He humbled Himself and became a man, He chose to operate out of His humanity, empowered by the Holy Spirit just as He expected His followers to do. After all, isn't that what He said? "Whoever believes in me will do the same things that I do. Those who believe will do even greater things than these, because I am going to the Father" (John 14:12 NCV).

The same Spirit who raised Jesus Christ from the dead dwells in us (see Romans 8:11). So if the Holy Spirit is the source of miracle-working power in the ministry and life of Jesus and I've got the same Spirit in me, then why am I not doing the same works that Jesus did and more?

I would love to see a man with a withered hand come into church and be able to tell him, "Stretch forth your hand!" and by the time he took it out of his jacket pocket, it would be totally restored by the power of God. I would love to see miracles—AIDS and cancer eradicated, quadriplegics walking. I know I have the God who does the impossible, and I have a burden to see what He can do.

ORDINARY FOLKS

When you read through the book of Acts, you find out that the apostles were doing such mighty works that people would come and worship them as if they were gods. That's what happened to Peter when he arrived at Cornelius's house (see Acts 10:25). These were ordinary men who were living such extraordinary lives that this sort of thing happened more than once, and each time they would have to say, "No, no, no! I am not God. I did not do this miracle!" and they would point the people to Jesus.

When was the last time you had the power of God operating through your life to such a degree that people wanted to worship you? I have not had that happen, and most likely you have not either. Most church people would object, "But, Pastor, of course we don't have that happen to us today. That happened only with the first apostles." To that, I suggest we look beyond the apostles for more examples. How about the man named Stephen and another man known as Philip? Both of these men were laymen, ordinary members of the church who had been elected as deacons. They were not apostles; in fact, they were servants in the Body of Christ—table-waiters.

Wherever Stephen went, miracles happened: "And Stephen, full of grace and power, did great wonders and signs among the people" (Acts 6:8 RSV). Eventually, he was arrested and persecuted because of this. In the end, when he was being stoned to death, he looked up and said, "Behold, I see the heavens opened, and the Son of man standing on the right hand of God" (Acts 7:56 KJV).

Philip was a good church member. He sat and listened to the apostles teach. His only official position in the church was to be a deacon, and he was always ready to serve in practical ways. Yet when he obeyed the voice of the Holy Spirit and went to a certain road where he encountered an Ethiopian man riding in a chariot and reading aloud from the book of Isaiah, and after he explained how Jesus Christ fulfilled those prophetic words, look what happened through him—and to him:

> *He* [a eunuch who served the queen of Ethiopia] *commanded the chariot to stop, and both of them, Philip and the eunuch, went down into the water, and Philip baptized him. When they came up out of the water, the Spirit of the Lord snatched Philip away; the eunuch saw him no more, and went on his way rejoicing. But Philip found himself at Azotus, and as he was passing through the region, he proclaimed the good news to all the towns until he came to Caesarea* (Acts 8:38-40 NRSV).

The eunuch's conversion and subsequent baptism in a small body of water alongside the road was just the beginning of amazing events. After that, the Spirit supernaturally whisked Philip to Azotus so that he could share the Good News in that region. Azotus was over thirty miles away!

Beside Stephen and Philip, we read about the exciting life of Paul, who had never met Jesus before His crucifixion and who had probably never met an apostle until after he was converted. He persecuted the new Church and by his own admission, he was "one born out of due season" (see 1 Corinthians 15:8). In other words, "I don't even deserve to be a servant of Jesus Christ. I don't have to come to you with a great message, but I can come to you with a demonstration of the Spirit and His power." That's just what he did, working miracle after miracle, year after year.

All through the Word of God we see ordinary people operating in the extraordinary power of God. Why are we not seeing these things today? Is it still true? Or is Jesus a liar along with everyone in the Bible? Is this book the biggest farce that humanity has ever fallen for? Or is it all true and we just haven't experienced it for ourselves yet?

THE SECRET OF THE THRONE ROOM

I believe the reason we don't have power is not because He is not still working but because we are out of line. Something is wrong with us. If we could discover what that might be, then we could unleash the power of God in our lives.

I believe we need to find a key to unlock the Kingdom. It has been right in front of us all along. Until Bible teacher and author Bob Sorge came to speak at my church, I did not fully understand what God has made available to us, how He has invited us into the sacred precincts of His very throne room. Bob preached about the secret place, God's throne room, and his message created a hunger in me to know all about it.

Look at what I found in the book of Hebrews:

Seeing then that we have a great high priest, that is passed into the heavens, Jesus the Son of God, let us hold fast our profession. For we have not an high priest which cannot be touched with the feeling of our infirmities; but was in all points tempted like as we are, yet without sin. Let us therefore come boldly unto the throne of grace, that we may obtain mercy, and find grace to help in time of need (Hebrews 4:14-16 KJV).

It's called the "throne of grace." We have an invitation to come to God's throne, which is where powerful mercy and grace come from. We are being invited to come. That's everybody—apostles, pastors, ordinary men and women. You and I have a personal invitation to visit the throne room of Heaven, the very throne room of God.

In Heaven there is a temple, a heavenly temple. We know this from the book of Revelation (chapters 2, 3, 4, 5, 17, and 19). The heavenly temple has an Outer Court, an Inner Court, and a Holy of Holies just like the temple of Solomon had here upon the earth, only the heavenly temple is much more extravagant.

God is saying, "I don't want you just to come to the Outer Court and stop there. I don't want you to come just to the Inner Court. I am inviting you to come to My very throne room, the holiest place of all." We have a personal invitation to enter the very throne room of God Almighty.

And as if that wasn't enough, He adds, "I don't want you to come based on the invitation alone, because I want you to come in a certain way. I want you to come boldly."

This would have been especially meaningful to the Jews who first received the book of Hebrews, because they knew that once a year on Yom Kippur their priests would take turns going into the Holy of Holies on behalf of the people. It was such a fearsome thing that the priest would walk backward into the Holy of Holies. There he would sprinkle blood upon the mercy seat. They knew that no man could see God and live, so they backed into the place.

Now here is God, inviting the people to whom He has extended mercy by the blood of the Savior Jesus to come right into the holiest place. He doesn't want people to back in—He wants them to barge in! He wants us to enter boldly, as if we belong there. We have special access that other people and other beings don't have.

It's something like this. If I were to visit my pastor and I needed a drink, I would say, "May I have a glass of water, please?" I wouldn't just barge in and grab a drink. However if I went into my family home as a son, I would never ask permission to have a glass of water. I would just go and get water or whatever I needed. My family would find it very strange if I were to ask permission.

According to the Word of God, you and I are heirs and joint heirs of Jesus Christ (see Romans 8:17). That means that whatever God would do for Jesus, God would do for me. God wants us to come boldly into the throne room of the throne of grace as if we own the place.

We come boldly to what kind of throne? This is a throne of *grace*. Now I know that everybody defines grace as "God's riches at Christ's expense," and there is truth to that. But in Strong's Concordance, the Greek word for *grace* carries a different definition: "Grace is divine influence that can be demonstrated in life."

That's why Paul can say, "I can demonstrate this Gospel." He wrote, "This extraordinary power belongs to God and does not come from us" (2 Corinthians 4:7 NRSV). Where did Paul get his miracle-working power? He got his extraordinary power to demonstrate the Gospel in action from the throne room—and he got it all the time.

ESCORTED TO THE THRONE ROOM

How can we come so boldly to the throne of grace? Only by the blood of the Savior, Jesus:

> *So, brothers and sisters, we are completely free to enter the Most Holy Place without fear because of the blood of Jesus' death. We can enter through a new and living way that Jesus opened for us. It leads through the curtain—Christ's body. And since we have a great priest over God's house, let us come near to God with a sincere heart and a sure faith, because we have been made free from a guilty conscience, and our bodies have been washed with pure water. Let us hold firmly to the hope that we have confessed, because we can trust God to do what he promised* (Hebrews 10:19-23 NCV).

We not only have an invitation, we also have an escort. Our escort is Jesus' blood, shed on the cross for us. We know this from the New Testament, but another way that we know it is from the book of Daniel. This is interesting; Daniel reported as follows: "I was watching in the night visions, and behold, One like the Son of Man, coming with the clouds of heaven! He came to the Ancient of Days, and they brought Him near before Him" (Daniel 7:13 NKJV). Notice the wording—"they brought Him near before Him."

Daniel had a vision or a dream in which he saw the Son of God coming with the clouds of Heaven to the Ancient of Days, which is another way of saying God the Father. And as you can see, Jesus had an escort: "they brought Him near before Him."

The question is this: who are *they*? Would ordinary people be escorting Him in? Absolutely not. Who could be escorting Him? Well, according to Ezekiel's vision (see Ezekiel chapters 10 and 11), the cherubim are always moving in Heaven, like a wheel in the middle of a wheel. I think it would be doctrinally correct to conclude that Jesus had an angelic escort to the Ancient of Days. So when Jesus approached the Father to put His blood on the mercy seat, He approached Him with an angelic escort.

Now, according to the passages from the book of Hebrews, we approach with a different escort. Our escort is not angelic. The children of the Most High God have a *blood* escort into the throne room. That blood that Jesus sprinkled on the mercy seat, His own blood, gives us complete access to the throne of grace. Because of His blood on the throne, now you and I do not require an angelic escort in order to get into the holiest place. We can go straight into the throne room, boldly. The blood makes the way. You don't hear much preaching about the blood anymore, but the blood is still the key to the throne of grace.

Grace is where divine influence can be demonstrated in a life. It is the source of power in the universe. In the spiritual power grid of the universe, the power plant for the grid is the throne of grace.

Not only do we have an invitation to enter the throne room, but we have a specific invitation to the holiest place in the universe, the holiest place of all: "Having therefore, brethren, boldness to enter into *the holiest* by the blood of Jesus…" (Hebrews 10:19 KJV). Wouldn't you think that the throne room was already the holiest place in the universe? It's not quite the holiest place, because the very holiest place is the bosom of the Father, Daddy's lap. (See John 1:18.) Jesus is in the bosom of the Father, heart of His heart, and that is the closest anyone can get to God.

So now not only do you have an invitation and a guaranteed escort to come into the throne room but, because of the blood of Jesus, you also have an invitation to get up into the throne and to sit in Daddy's lap.

The question is this: do you believe it? If it sounds too far out for you, you will deprive yourself of access to the power of God. To repeat—there is only one source of spiritual power, and that is the very throne of God. Authority comes from God Almighty Himself and nobody else. You cannot just decide to say, "I am going to get up and do a miracle." That's not how it works. But if God says, "You are going to get up and do a miracle," a miracle will happen. He determines the miracles.

HEAVENLY PLACES

The heavenly Father is inviting you to sit with Him just as Jesus sits with Him. That's what the Word tells us—that we are seated in heavenly places in Christ Jesus:

> *Though we were spiritually dead because of the things we did against God, he gave us new life with Christ. You have been saved by God's grace. And he raised us up with Christ and gave us a seat with him in the heavens. He did this for those in Christ Jesus so that for all future time he could show the very great riches of his grace by being kind to us in Christ Jesus. I mean that you have been saved by grace through believing. You did not save yourselves; it was a gift from God. It was not the result of your own efforts, so you cannot brag about it. God has made us what we are. In Christ Jesus, God made us to do good works, which God planned in advance for us to live our lives doing* (Ephesians 2:5-10 NCV).

I have always tended to see God—the Father, the Son, and the Holy Spirit—at work in the universe, but I have seen myself way down here on earth. I've heard about the angels flying around the cherubim singing, "Holy, holy, holy," and thunder and lightning and all of that in the throne room. (You can read about it in Revelation 4 and 5.) Yet, I have always viewed myself as standing way down here, far away (and in some ways thankful to be so far away!).

That's not what Jesus died for. He didn't come and die just so we could remain far away. Jesus died to get us into Daddy's lap.

When I was a kid, one of my favorite things to do was to get off the bus at my grandmother and granddaddy's house. They had an old house with a front porch. I would run up that long driveway across the field, and my granddaddy would be sitting in the chair on the front porch. My favorite thing to do was to run up the steps and jump up into his arms, where I could sit in his lap and talk with him about how my day had gone. That's a picture of how it is with you and the Father. Yet here's what we do in the Church: we say, "Lord, send Your power down. Lord, come down to us. Lord, come."

God is answering, "Hold it. I ripped the veil, not so I could come down to you, but so that you could come up here to Me. Come on up now." We always want Him to come down and we do not seem to want to go to the heavenly places in Christ Jesus. Why do we always want to live down here? We freely ask God to get involved down here. But all the while He is seated far above all principalities and powers, far above everything that is in the earth, all powers, all might, all dominion. He does not want you to invite Him to come down. He wants to invite you to come up!

The Bible says that Jesus sits at the Father's right hand. When Stephen was being stoned, where did he see Jesus? At the right hand of the Father. (See Acts 7:56.) Psalm 110 pictures Jesus at the right hand of the Father as well. But according to Psalm 109:31, the Lord is at *my* right hand: "For He shall stand at the right hand of the poor, to save him from those who condemn him." I am poor and so are you—weak and easily defeated. Yet, I have been positioned in heavenly places, right in the bosom of the Father.

Every time I go into the throne room, I am transfixed by its magnificence. The thunder and lightning, the sound, the angels zooming around. However, that's not what Jesus shed His blood for—so that I could come and look at angels. I get to go past the angels who cry, "Holy," and I get to crawl up into the throne of God. (First Peter 1:12 says that the angels desire to look into redemption. They don't have a blood escort.) When I get to the seat of the throne, there is Daddy God. I hug Him and say, "Daddy, I love You." I start talking to Him. Then I turn to His right hand and hug Jesus, and I tell Him I love Him, too. They say, "Sit with us." Then the three of us sit together in the heavenly throne of grace.

There's plenty of room there, and all the time in the world. Doesn't it make you want to come up too? You really love Jesus. Why stay down here dreaming about one day coming up to heavenly places, when in Jesus you can come there right now?

PRAYING IN THE THRONE ROOM

That brings us to prayer. Knowing about the throne room and the Father's lap has redefined my prayer life. Jesus said, in essence, "Don't pray like other people pray" (see Matthew 6). He said, "Don't pray with long repetition. Don't use all of those religious slogans. When you pray, go into your secret place, lock yourself in with the Father, and talk with Him."

In your own prayer time, you can get into a heavenly position in Christ through His blood. Go and be seated with Him in heavenly places. Spend your prayer time listening to what the Father is saying to the Son and what the Son is saying to the Father. There have been times when I have heard them talking to each other, and I understood what they wanted me to do. Every time I have done that thing they told me to do, I have seen miracles. That almost sounds like something Jesus would say, doesn't it? "Jesus said, 'I tell you the truth, the Son can do nothing alone. The Son does only what he sees the Father doing, because the Son does whatever the Father does'" (John 5:19 NCV). I want to stay close to God so that I can't say or do anything except what He has said and done first.

The key to such power is in the throne room, and the reason the Church doesn't have any power is because we keep asking God to come down here and demonstrate Himself. The whole time God is saying, "No, you come up here and get in the throne of divine influence, so you can demonstrate My power in the earth as My Son did."

So holy is the bosom of the Father that we are changed when we spend time there. No one can ever stay the same if they spend time right in the middle of the communion and compassion of the Trinity. I have learned how to live up there for the most part. Every morning, the first thing I say is, "Lord, sprinkle me with Your blood. I have failed you. I have come far short of Your glory, but Jesus' blood makes me whiter than snow. You have said that if I confess my sin, You will be faithful and just to forgive my sin and to cleanse me from all unrighteousness. Sprinkle me with Your blood."

I feel the cleansing power of that blood. I'm sure you have had times when you have asked Him for forgiveness and you felt as if somebody was literally pouring cleansing fluid over you. You can feel yourself being washed clean. Whether or not I feel it every time, I say to Him, "Lord, now I know that I am righteous in You, because of Your blood. Now I can accept Your invitation to come into the holiest place in the universe." Then, I step boldly into Heaven, just as confidently as I used to come home from college and run through the front door and say, "Momma! Daddy! I'm back!"

This is the real Christian life and not the life of deism that most so-called Christians live. For the most part, the Church is full of people who are deists in their thinking. They recognize that there is this big God up there who is in charge of everything, but they don't realize that He is personally involved in their lives. More than that, they don't realize that they have been invited to join Him in Heaven—before they die.

Once you try it, you will understand how you can't go back to your old way of doing things. Go boldly into the throne room even if the people around you think you are crazy. Nobody may comprehend your throne room experiences but you. But it is a fact that the throne room is not an ethereal, imaginary place. It's a real place that you can go to anytime you want.

There is no stress there. It's only when you come out that you get stressed. For example, this morning in the shower I said, "Lord, sprinkle me with Your blood. I want to go into the throne room, and I want to be with You." I did that. Then I had to go to the airport and things started going crazy. I started freaking out. I felt myself go whooshing out of the place of total peace in God, almost like a vacuum had sucked me out of that heavenly place and spit me out back down in this natural realm. Then I boarded the plane and realized what had happened. I said again, "Lord, sprinkle me with Your blood. I want to go back to that heavenly place." I simply went back to the throne room. I have been learning to stay longer each time. When I first started trying to live there, I would get sucked out all the time because I wasn't used to living there. By now, I've practiced the presence of God enough that I've learned to live there more of the time.

A humble Christian named Brother Lawrence wrote a little book in the seventeenth century called *The Practice of the Presence of God*. He found that he could live in the presence of God twenty-four hours a day, seven days a week. Jesus became our Savior so that all of us could have this experience. I have lived here, and I have lived up there. Up there is better.

DWELL IN THE SECRET PLACE— AND SEE MIRACLES

Have you ever found yourself in a church service where God's presence just broke out? If you have, you know how it feels to be saturated in God's peace. You don't worry about your kids or about money. You are not really doing anything; you're just sitting there. When you have such an experience, you have tasted what it is like to get into the bosom of the Father. When you walked out of the church, you may have thought you had to leave it behind. You didn't. You can live there twenty-four hours a day, seven days a week. Living there will give you abundant peace—and some miracles, too.

Not long ago, I went to Mississippi because I had been asked to preach at a church. A lady came forward in the church service. When she came up to the front, I could see that her right eye was milky white. She said, "I can't see and I want to see. I can distinguish light and dark, but I can't see anything else."

Because for several weeks I had been spending extra time in this heavenly place in Christ, I immediately heard the Father say to the Son, "Tell the eye to look straight on." I was standing there in front of her, but it was like I was also seated in the heavenly place of the throne room.

I had twenty-five students with me, young adults who are in a college program we have at our church. I called them over and told them, "For the first time in my ministry—the first time in twenty years of preaching full time—I know this woman is getting ready to receive a creative miracle. I know she is going to get healed, and I want you to see it with your own eyes." They gathered around. I told the woman to put her left hand over her other eye, and then I said, "The Lord said, 'Tell the eye to look straight on.'" As soon as I said those words—and I didn't lay hands on her; I didn't blow on her; I didn't yell; I didn't scream—her milky eye started to form a pupil and an iris! Then I could see it focus. She started screaming and shouting to God. It scared the students to death. They had never seen anything like it. Some of them ran backward.

Now, do you know what we do at our church? All of our people are learning to spend time in the throne room. We tell them to go to work every day and just do whatever they hear God say. We witness that way.

We also have what we call Treasure Hunts. We got the idea from Kevin Dedmon from Bethel Church in Redding, California.

HEAVEN IS A PLACE WHERE YOU CAN GO NOW

The Bible tells us not to "give place" to the devil (see Ephesians 4:27). Place. Not opportunity, but *place*. Don't ever forget that Heaven is a place. It's a real place. That's why Jesus could ascend to it, and that's why we can, too, in response to God's invitation.

Did you know that even Judas had a place saved for him in God's throne room? According to chapters four and five of the book of Revelation, twenty-four thrones surround the throne of God. Why twenty-four? Twelve for the heads of the twelve tribes of Israel and twelve for the apostles Jesus chose. That represents twelve of the Old Covenant and twelve of the New Covenant.

But we learn in Acts 1:20 that Judas made his place "desolate." Luke was quoting Psalm 69:25. The Lord had chosen Judas as one of the apostles; therefore Judas had been assigned one of those thrones. But he vacated his seat. He gave up his place. The enemy has one desire, and that is to take you out of your place in God.

Remember: "He that dwelleth in the secret place of the most High shall abide under the shadow of the Almighty" (Psalm 91:1 KJV). When you are in the bosom of the Father, the devil can't get to you. In the Father's lap is the holiest place in the universe. However, if the devil can get you to climb out of Daddy's lap, he can persuade you to abandon your place, your secret place.

I can't tell you what the throne room is going to look like for you. I thank God that it is personal for every individual. I can tell you that in that place is fullness and joy and peace that passes all understanding, power, and authority. It doesn't matter whether you are sitting or standing or walking when you enter into the secret place in prayer. For myself, I like to stand up. You can choose whatever position is most comfortable for you. And you can do it anytime.

If after a time in the throne room you begin to feel as though you have been sucked out, you can get back in. You may feel the weight of the world coming back onto you. The world is heavy. Life is heavy. Let me tell you what I have learned to do. Whenever that happens, even in public, I find a quiet place to pray. I say, "Lord, sprinkle me with Your blood. I'm sorry I left." Then go right back into it. It will take you about five minutes.

I have learned that wrong words will pull me out of that holy place quicker than anything else. If you find yourself gossiping, you will be sucked out immediately. If you are around somebody who uses the name of the Lord in vain you will be pulled down. Certain things pull each person out of that place.

Every time, just go and ask Him to sprinkle you with His blood so you can go right back into that sacred place. Eventually, you will learn to live there twenty-four hours a day, seven days a week.

You were created to live there. What you feel when you are there is what Adam and Eve felt all day long, even in the midst of working and tending the Garden. The real you is a spirit, and it was created to live in a spiritual place.

—∽∽—

Right now, you can step into the throne room—

Father, I thank You that You have given me an invitation to come into Your throne room, into the holiest place in the universe, the bosom of the Father. But Lord, I am not worthy to come to that place because of the things I have done and the things I have not done, things that You told me to do. So, Lord, I need You right now to sprinkle me with Your blood. Let Your love flow over me. Cleanse me. Now that I am righteous by the blood, help me to make my way to the throne room. Let me see You there on the throne.

Let me climb up into Your lap, Daddy, and hug You. Let me gaze upon You and tell You what I think about You. Let me thank Jesus for making it possible. Now I can stay here, or return anytime I want to. No worry. No pain. No struggle. Amen!

Chapter 11

THE PATHWAY TO DOMINION

*The heaven, even the heavens, are the
Lord's; but the earth He has given to the
children of men* (PSALM 115:16).

When God created the plants that grow all over the earth, He did it by speaking to the dirt: "God said, 'Let the earth put forth vegetation, plants yielding seed, and fruit trees bearing fruit in which is their seed, each according to its kind, upon the earth.' And it was so" (Genesis 1:11 RSV).

Then when God wanted to make birds, He spoke to the air they would be flying through. When He made the first animals, He spoke to the ground they would walk and crawl over. Accordingly, when God created fish, He spoke to the water they would swim in. He always used a *source* for His creation. As Myles Munroe wrote on page 21 of his book, *Understanding Your Potential,* "All things have the same source components and essence as their source. What God created is, in essence, like the substance from which it came."

When the time came for God to create humans, the same creative formula applied. However, this time He did not speak to the dirt, the air, or the water. When He created the first man, God spoke directly to *Himself*. God created man by speaking to Himself! This shows us that in the very beginning, God was taking something from Himself and putting it into Adam so that Adam would be like Him and share in His life:

> *Then God said, "Let Us make man in Our image, according to Our likeness; let them have dominion over the fish of the sea, over the birds of the air, and over the cattle, over all the earth and over every creeping thing that creeps on the earth."*
> *...Then God blessed them, and God said to them, "Be fruitful and multiply; fill the earth and subdue it; have dominion over the fish of the sea, over the birds of the air, and over every living thing that moves on the earth"* (Genesis 1:26,28).

DOMINION

Once God had created Adam and placed him in the Garden of Eden, He gave Adam legal dominion over the earth. Although Satan had once been the "anointed cherub" who had covered the earth, now, because of his rebellion, God took that glorious position away from him and gave it to Adam and to his descendants. He anointed human beings to rule the earth instead of Satan.

Psalm 82:6 (RSV) declares, "I say, 'You are gods, sons of the Most High, all of you.'" In a very real sense, we can say that the Lord made humankind, beginning with Adam and Eve, to be the gods of this world. Of course, that statement needs some clarification. Adam and Eve were not gods in the sense of being divine beings, but they were made to be gods in the sense of their godlike authority or dominion. In His creative order, God put Adam and Eve in authority so that they could dominate the earth.

At the time of the creation of Adam and Eve, the Garden of Eden did not cover the entire earth. "And the Lord God planted a garden eastward in Eden; and there he put the man whom he had formed" (Genesis 2:8 KJV). God gave them the responsibility to tend the garden, to dominate it, and to multiply it until it covers the earth. God's eternal plan is still the same. This desire to see the earth as an all-encompassing garden will one day be realized when God unveils the new Heaven and new earth. "The heaven, even the heavens, are the Lord's; but the earth He has given to the children of men" (Psalm 115:16).

God literally gave the earth to the human beings He had created. The great Creator of the heavens and the earth gave us the power and authority to rule over the earth. Unfortunately, Satan, having once ruled over the earth himself and being angry about his displacement, saw a great opportunity to regain his position. He could see that unconditional authority had been delegated to these upstarts, so he tempted them to surrender that authority by directly disobeying God's commands. As we know, they fell for Satan's ploy. When Adam and Eve disobeyed God, another transfer of dominion took place. (This is not the same as ownership, because the earth belongs to the Lord God forever.) Dominion was handed back to Satan, at least temporarily. At that point Satan became "the god of this world" who "has blinded the minds of the unbelievers, to keep them from seeing the light of the gospel of the glory of Christ, who is the image of God" (2 Corinthians 4:4 NRSV). Humankind lost control from that point forward. Death had entered the world through one man's disobedience.

In the long run, however, God took care of the situation. He sent His Son Jesus Christ to the earth as a man to restore rightful dominion to the beings He had created in His own image. For thirty-three years Jesus walked this earth, totally yielded to the Holy Spirit and submitted to God the Father. Not once did He capitulate to temptation and relinquish His heavenly position. "For we do not have a High Priest who cannot sympathize with our weaknesses, but was in all points tempted as we are, yet without sin" (Hebrew 4:15). By virtue of the atoning work of the cross, Jesus, through obedience unto death (see Philippians 2:8), reclaimed and restored humankind's legal right to dominion.

Some of our Lord's final words are as follows:

> *And Jesus came and spake unto them, saying, All power is given unto me in heaven and in earth. Go ye therefore, and teach all nations, baptizing them in the name of the Father, and of the Son, and of the Holy Ghost: teaching them to observe all things whatsoever I have commanded you: and, lo, I am with you always, even unto the end of the world. Amen* (Matthew 28:18-20 KJV).

Go ye implies that the dominion and authority that belong to our Lord has been transferred to every believer in Jesus Christ. Whoever calls Him "Lord" now represents Him on earth. Amazingly, because of the Lord's redemptive work, every believer has been "made...alive together with Christ (by grace you have been saved), and raised us up together, and made us sit together in the heavenly places in Christ Jesus" (Ephesians 2:5-6).

All Christians have been raised up and seated with Christ, even while they still remain here upon the earth. The physical position of believing men and women does not change, but their spiritual position does! Now, in Him, all of them are seated "Far above all rule and authority and power and dominion and every name that is named [above every title that can be conferred], not only in this age and in this world, but also in the age and the world which are to come" (Ephesians 1:21 AMP).

WORSHIP IS THE KEY TO SPIRITUAL DOMINION

What does the believer's spiritual position have to do with the subject of worship? Because Satan was created as a worshipping angel to have dominion over this earth, and because Christians are his replacement, worship has everything to do with it! Worship was Satan's pathway to dominion (as well as his pathway out of dominion). In the same way, worship is also every believer's pathway in—and out—of dominion. When Adam and Eve disobeyed, thereby ceasing to worship God through obedience, they lost their authority. On the other hand, when Jesus, the God-man, worshipped God through total obedience, He regained authority for humankind; He sacrificed Himself to win people back to their full status as His co-regents over the earth God created.

Because Satan was created as a worshipping angel and then was given authority over the earth, it follows that worship must be a key to spiritual dominion.

PRAISE CHOKES THE ENEMY

There is another clue to our destiny as the ones whose destiny is to exercise God's dominion over the earth:

> *Judah, your brothers shall praise you; your hand shall be on the neck of your enemies; your father's sons shall bow down before you. Judah is a lion's whelp; from the prey, my son, you have gone up. He stooped down, he couched as a lion, and as a lioness; who dares rouse him up? The scepter shall not depart from Judah, nor the ruler's staff from between his feet, until he comes to whom it belongs; and to him shall be the obedience of the peoples (Genesis 49:8-10 RSV).*

This passage is rich with truth that connects worship with spiritual authority. The name *Judah* means "praise" in the Hebrew language. When one reads this passage and substitutes the word *praise* for Judah, the authority factor of worship becomes easily apparent. For example, verse ten declares that the scepter shall not depart from Judah. A scepter is an ornamented staff or rod that has long represented authority. Translated accordingly, this verse declares, "Authority shall not depart from praise." Verse eight states that Judah's "hand shall be on the neck of your enemies." Again, you can see the authority factor of worship. Translated accurately, it would read, "Praise...your hand shall be on the neck of your enemies." As a believer, do you understand what this statement means? Your praise to God can choke out any enemy that Satan tries to use against your rightful position as a child of God!

This same principle is illustrated in Judges 20:18 (NCV), "The Israelites went up to the city of Bethel and asked God, 'Which tribe shall be first to attack the Benjaminites?' The Lord answered, 'Judah shall go first.' Here we see that Judah—praise—went into battle first. This shows that worship is a weapon of warfare that must precede everything else. Worship is primary. Until a believer grasps this revelation, he or she will be overwhelmed with oppression and satanic opposition.

In other words, the pathway to exercising our rightful dominion and authority is through the warfare of worship.

One day, when I was in the throes of one of my worst personal struggles, I was listening to a podcast by Bill Johnson, who is an insightful man of God and a well-known pastor in Redding, California. He made a statement that confirmed what God was already saying to me at that time about worship: "We must learn to work out of rest and to wage warfare out of worship." This is a supremely powerful spiritual principle! Worship chokes the enemy to death; it represents one of the primary scepters of authority that has been given to every believer and to the Body of Christ as a whole.

Satan hates worship! The enemy of our souls knows what worship does in the heavens—how it affects God, how it affects the worshipper, and of course how it affects him. He knows all too well that revelation about and application of worship comprise a spiritual weapon with which he cannot reckon. Worship renders him helpless.

I hope by now that every believer who is reading this book is starting to connect the dots concerning why worship is so significant. Never forget the effect of worship in the spirit realm and the authority it pours into the life of the believer.

Chapter 12

RESTORING THE
TABERNACLE OF DAVID

*"On that day I will raise up the tabernacle of David,
which has fallen down, and repair its damages; I
will raise up its ruins, and rebuild it as in the days
of old; that they may possess the remnant of Edom,
and all the Gentiles who are called by My name,"
says the Lord who does this thing* (Amos 9:11-12).

Yºu will remember from Chapter 2 that the tabernacle of David was a
special tent that was made by David to house Moses' Ark of the Covenant (which had been housed in earlier times by the tabernacle of Moses,
and Moses' tabernacle foreshadowed the temple in its design). Whereas
the style of worship in the tabernacle of Moses had involved animal sacrifices, the style of worship in David's tabernacle was different. David
instructed the people to come in—everyone was allowed to come in, not

only the priests—and make *sacrifices of praise* or joyful songs of thanksgiving to God for His greatness and mercy.

The Davidic sacrifices of praise have never been replaced among God's people, although they have been sorely neglected. I believe that we are seeing in this day a restoration of the tabernacle of David, a revival of true worship and a resurgence of the many ramifications of Davidic worship.

The prophet Amos prophesied that the tabernacle of David would be restored, and the apostle James quoted him in the presence of the leaders of the early church:

> *James answered, saying, "Men and brethren, listen to me: Simon has declared how God at the first visited the Gentiles to take out of them a people for His name. And with this the words of the prophets agree, just as it is written: 'After this I will return and will rebuild the tabernacle of David, which has fallen down; I will rebuild its ruins, and I will set it up; so that the rest of mankind may seek the Lord, even all the Gentiles who are called by My name, says the Lord who does all these things'"* (Acts 15:13-17, quoting Amos 9:11).

A controversy surrounds the interpretation of this passage. Some people believe that the tabernacle of David refers to the original Davidic kingdom and its future reestablishment on the earth. Others believe that it refers to an end-time reemergence of the Davidic order of worship. I believe it refers to both, and that the most active application for our purposes concerns the revival of the Davidic practices of worship.

OLD TESTAMENT TO NEW

All through the New Testament and therefore, throughout the history of the Church, the theme of Davidic worship is strong. John wrote that Jesus had tabernacled among us (see John 1:14). The new church is called the "temple of God (see 1 Corinthians 3:16; Ephesians 2:19-22). Songs and hymns and spiritual songs speak of "Zion," "God's holy temple," and "the mountain of the Lord," all of which refer to the placement of David's tabernacle on Mount Zion in Jerusalem.

Those who have eyes to see and ears to hear and hearts to perceive know that a tremendous move of the Holy Spirit has been promised to the world and to the Church in the last days, and we are seeing evidence of His work. At the present time, Jesus, the head of the Church, is emphasizing specific spiritual truths in order to mature His Church and to bring it like a bride into proper spiritual alignment so that He can "present...to himself a glorious church, not having spot, or wrinkle, or any such thing; but that it should be holy and without blemish" (Ephesians 5:27 KJV).

One of the great emphases of the last days before the Lord's coming is the divine order of worship. Because human beings have been created to worship but they suffer from ignorance and lack of discernment about God's ways, they tend to worship the wrong things in the wrong ways. I see a real need to discover what the Word of God says about the matter. God promises that worship will be a major key to the last-day moving of the Spirit, and we can summarize the reasons as follows:

- Worship develops a strong, tough spirit.

- Worship polishes the life of the believer.

- Worship reveals the nature and holiness of God's character.

- Worship is the foundation of the believer's walk with God.

- Worship provides protection from enemies.

- Worship creates a habitation for God.

- Worship gives the believer discernment of the times and seasons.

Worship is not just something that we do on Sunday mornings when we gather together in our churches. *Worshippers* equals our identity as believers—worshippers of the Triune God who cannot help but praise Him, pray to Him, and proclaim His mighty strength everywhere we go. God wants us as worshippers not to merely regurgitate somebody else's worship songs or sounds. He wants us to participate with His Holy Spirit to restore prior songs and worship sounds and to create all-new ones.

SONGS OF PRAISE, PRAYER, AND PROCLAMATION

I am passionate about the restoration of David's tabernacle, and I know that in order for all of us to participate in the restoration of the tabernacle of David we need to take a look at the book of Psalms, because they are the songs that were composed to be used in the original Davidic worship.

The psalms were written to be sung aloud to the accompaniment of musical instruments. The instrumentation is as important as the voicing of the lyrics. Every time the words and melodies and cadences of one of the psalms rings out, a clear message is released into the atmosphere, a message that almost always falls into one of three categories—Prayer, Proclamation, or Praise.

Many of the psalms have come down to us with their original musical and literary notations intact. At the beginning of Psalm 17, for example, you will see the words, "A prayer of David." This is an example of a prayer-psalm. The words express the speaker/singer's heartfelt desires toward God:

> *Hear a just cause, O Lord; attend to my cry; give ear to my prayer from lips free of deceit. From you let my vindication*

come.... I call upon you, for you will answer me, O God; incline your ear to me, hear my words. Wondrously show your steadfast love, O savior of those who seek refuge from their adversaries at your right hand. Guard me as the apple of the eye; hide me in the shadow of your wings (Psalm 17:1-2,6-8 NRSV).

In the previous psalm, Psalm 16, we find the notation, "A Miktam of David." This is another way of saying "A proclamation of David." The words of the song proclaim and declare the goodness and faithfulness of a dependable and loving God:

The Lord is my chosen portion and my cup; you hold my lot. The boundary lines have fallen for me in pleasant places; I have a goodly heritage. ...Therefore my heart is glad, and my soul rejoices; my body also rests secure. ...You show me the path of life. In your presence there is fullness of joy; in your right hand are pleasures forevermore (Psalm 16:5-6,9,11 NRSV).

Most of the psalms are songs of praise. Nobody knows the original tunes anymore, but many of them have been set to new music over the centuries. Paul urged the people of God to sing "psalms and hymns and spiritual songs" continually (see Ephesians 5:18-19 and Colossians 3:16). Besides David's psalms, he wanted the people to compose new songs—and to enter a dimension of praise that he called *spiritual songs.*

Spiritual songs resonate at a frequency that the human spirit and the Holy Spirit can hear. Without the Spirit, they cannot be sung. They are new, even when they are based on the songs of previous generations, and they are powerful even when they are whispered. In the days to come, when we are part of the new Heaven and new earth, all of the music will be new spiritual songs. (I can hardly wait.)

STRIKE UP THE INSTRUMENTS

David was a skilled musician, and he seems to have been able to play several of the instruments of his day. Accordingly, his psalms often carry notations regarding their preferred instrumentation. For example, at the head of Psalm 4 we find something like this (depending on which version you are reading): "To the choirmaster: with stringed instruments; a psalm of David," or "To the chief musician on Neginoth; a psalm of David." (*Neginoth* means "stringed instruments"; the same note is found also on Psalm 76.) In other words, when David wrote this song, he knew it would work best when accompanied by stringed instruments. In fact, I think you could go so far as to say that the anointing on the psalm would not be effective without the stringed instruments.

This leads to other possible conclusions. David played something called a twenty-two-string harp. Interestingly, the Hebrew alphabet has twenty-two letters. The idea of playing a harp or other stringed instrument involves plucking, striking, or twanging the strings individually. When David played the twenty-two-string harp, he could have been spelling out words in Hebrew, or creating alphabetical lyrics by means of his music. If you consider that far-fetched, just think about times when you have been in a worship setting and a particular song started to reach your spirit in a fresh way; God spoke to you through the words or the arrangement of the music. In those situations, He was superimposing His voice and His words upon the musical notes, and in your spirit you understood what He was saying.

The musical instructions for Psalm 6 ask for "stringed instruments according to the Sheminith." The Sheminith is an eight-stringed harp or lyre. Psalm 12 carries the same instructions. Verse 9 of Psalm 144 calls for a harp of ten strings. Each one of those instruments speaks in a different voice and that voice penetrates to a different dimension. Sometimes, if you combine the instruments, you break into a new dimension.

As I explained in Chapter 1 at the beginning of this book, a new sound breaks an old cycle. Worship is powerful!

Here's another one. Psalm 8 begins with these words: "To the choirmaster; according to The Gittith. A Psalm of David." What does *The Gittith* mean? It appears in two other psalm titles, and it seems to have something to do with Gath, which is where the Philistine giant Goliath came from. Quite possibly, this psalm was meant to be played on an instrument that had been looted from the conquered Philistines of Gath. According to one of the *targumim,* the oral explanations of the Talmud that the rabbis would provide for the Jews, this was the name of a harp that David had brought back from Gath after his great success in warfare. Needless to say, we no longer can play Psalm 8 in quite the same way as it was written!

Psalm 5 carries this notation: "To the choirmaster: for the flutes; a psalm of David" ("To the chief musician on Nehiloth; a psalm of David"). *Nehiloth* means "flutes." To worship using that psalm, the musicians laid aside their harps and took up their wind instruments. Another psalm that does not involve harps is Psalm 39, which directs "to Jeduthun" who was one of David's chief musicians, a man who played the trumpet and the cymbals.

All of this makes me think of the way that bluegrass or jazz musicians take turns playing solos. First one of the stringed instruments like the fiddle or the string bass will take center stage, then maybe a horn, and sometimes even the drums. I think God likes it when we take turns because He has an anointing for each one of us to release a new sound. He wants us to be able to step forward at the right time and play the right song and focus on a particular chord progression, a riff, or a single note. We can stay on our solo as long as the presence of God is on it, and when we feel His presence lift we can step back and let the next musician take over. We aren't used to doing that as much as we used to be. These days most worship musicians all play at the same time; they "jam."

When I really started getting into this, I also noticed the instructions on Psalm 22, which read as follows: "To the chief musician upon Aijeleth Shahar, a psalm of David," or "To the choirmaster; according to The Hind of the Dawn; a psalm of David." What is "The Hind of the Dawn"? It is not an instrument. It is a tune, a known melody. So David must have done what a lot of the more recent hymn writers have done; he must have taken a melody that was popular in the culture in Israel at the time and co-opted it for use as religious music. Each psalm or song had a specified purpose. A little later in the collection of psalms, we find a notation (on Psalm 38): "for the memorial offering," or "to bring to remembrance." That psalm is a penitent's plea for mercy, "God, remember me in my miserable condition."

One more: at the beginning of Psalm 46 we see the words, "According to Alamoth," which means "young woman"—in other words, a soprano. For that song, the male musicians were being instructed to use high falsetto voices!

CELEBRATING THE RETURN OF THE ARK

When King David, after a long wait and a major setback, managed to engineer the return of the Ark of the Covenant to Jerusalem where it would be installed in his new tabernacle, his celebratory caravan was accompanied by a large number of singers and instrumentalists. Picture this scene:

> *David also commanded the chiefs of the Levites to appoint their kindred as the singers to play on musical instruments, on harps and lyres and cymbals, to raise loud sounds of joy. ...The singers Heman, Asaph, and Ethan were to sound bronze cymbals; Zechariah, Aziel, Shemiramoth, Jehiel, Unni, Eliab, Maaseiah, and Benaiah were to play harps according to Alamoth; but Mattithiah, Eliphelehu, Mikneiah, Obed-edom, Jeiel, and Azaziah were to lead with lyres according to the Sheminith. Chenaniah, leader of*

the Levites in music, was to direct the music, for he under-stood it. Berechiah and Elkanah were to be gatekeepers for the ark. Shebaniah, Joshaphat, Nethanel, Amasai, Zechariah, Benaiah, and Eliezer, the priests, were to blow the trumpets before the ark of God... (1 Chronicles 15:16,19-24 NRSV).

This was not just a holiday parade. The combined sound of the orchestration was designed to break down invisible spiritual barriers and carry the people into heavenly realms. To this day, the Jews repeat some of these songs, because they still believe in the efficacy of "getting it right" in prayer and singing.

LIVING IN THE CLOSING DAYS OF GRACE

We are living in the closing days of grace, and one universal need permeates the Body of Christ—the need for discernment. This is why many voices in the Church are speaking up to remind us about the wisdom of the "sons of Issachar." Who were they?

First Chronicles 12:32 (RSV) explains that the sons of Issachar were "men who had understanding of the times, to know what Israel ought to do." Discernment, Issachar's greatest asset, seems to be the Church's greatest deficiency in the present day. Without discernment, the Body of Christ wanders, in grave danger of being overtaken by deceiving spirits and demonic doctrines (see 1 Timothy 4:1) and in danger of missing its moment of visitation (see Luke 19:44).

From reading Numbers 2:5 and Numbers 10:14-15, we know that the tribe of Issachar camped around the tabernacle under the standard of Judah (which means "praise"), thus instituting a correlation between worshipful praise and discernment. Just as the children of Issachar must have developed their discernment out of their relationship with praise, it seems to me that a proper revelation of praise and worship today equips the Church with discernment for the last days.

Scriptural descriptions of the vestments of the ancient high priests depict the breastplate as being adorned with twelve stones, each stone representing one of the twelve tribes of Israel. Each stone was a different color, and each stone had the name of a tribe inscribed upon it. Issachar's stone was a sapphire. The sapphire is mentioned twelve times in the Bible. The best-known variety of sapphire has blue tints, but sapphires exist in all the colors of the rainbow. The sapphire is second only to the diamond in hardness. For this reason, the stone is often used as an abrasive or polishing agent. Many Bible scholars believe that the sapphire represents the Lord's divine nature and His holy character as seen in Exodus 24:10, Ezekiel 1:26, 10:1, and Revelation 21:19. (In both Exodus and Ezekiel, the descriptions of sapphire under the Lord's feet signify that the very foundation of all that the Lord does is built upon His divine nature and holy character.)

It is the heritage of the saints of God to receive the sure mercies of David (see Isaiah 55:3, Acts 13:34) including protection from enemies (see Isaiah 54:17), the potential to become joint heirs (see Romans 8:17), and the opportunity to become the habitation of God (see Ephesians 2:22). The Spirit of holiness (see Psalm 89:34-36) confirmed this heritage to David. Such a heritage also advances holiness in the hearts of those who believe in God. Isaiah 54:11 shows that the sapphire is part of the basic foundation of a strong house or city that can withstand onslaughts, because it represents the divine nature and holy character of God. Only upon this same foundation of holiness and character can successful Christian life be built.

WHERE ARE MY KEYS?

Both the Davidic kingdom and the Davidic order of worship are emerging in the earth during these final days of grace. Psalm 43:3 (KJV) speaks of multiple tabernacles, "O send out thy light and thy truth: let them lead me; let them bring me unto thy holy hill, and to thy tabernacles." Psalm 84:1 again emphasizes multiple tabernacles, "How amiable are thy tabernacles, O Lord of hosts." This is one way we can see that the Davidic throne cannot be separated from Davidic worship; they are divinely connected. Even David's selection to be king of Israel came as a direct result of his worship while he tended his father's sheep, followed by his victory over Goliath. Not only did David scorn Goliath's reproach of the God of Israel, he made sure that his entire kingship was characterized by worship.

To this day, David's kingdom is renowned even though his establishment of the tabernacle for worship is less well known. Still, the book of Revelation describes the reestablishment of the future Davidic kingdom through Jesus' rule. The throne of David will always be connected to the throne of worship (see Revelation 19). This divine connection opens the mystery of the "key of David" (Revelation 3:7).

God promises to pour out His Spirit upon all flesh in the last days. This outpouring began on the day of Pentecost (see Acts 2), but the day will come when the Holy Spirit will be poured out on all flesh like the former and the latter rain together. The day of Pentecost was just the beginning of the outpouring; the power of God's presence is going to come upon all flesh someday. It is not by chance that there is such a simultaneous emphasis in modern Christendom on worship and also on the rediscovery of the church's Jewish roots. The purpose of the tabernacle of David and the reestablishment of the Davidic order of worship is to usher in the outpouring of the Holy Ghost in the last days. The merging of revelatory streams is positioning the Church with the key of David for Kingdom work around the earth.

What must we do to possess the key of David? It is not difficult; we must come to understand the power of praise and worship as it relates to the establishment of the Kingdom of God on this earth. As the Church learns to pattern worship after the tabernacle of David, the people of God will find the key to the harvest of nations.

Acts 15 gives an account of a gathering of apostles and elders at Jerusalem to discuss the matter of Judaizing teachers of the Law of Moses who had sought to bring believing Gentiles under the bondage of the Law. The Gentiles were coming to a saving faith in Jesus Christ, but the Judaizers wanted them to observe and practice the Law of Moses. The decisions of the apostles would affect the future of the New Testament Church and the relationship between Jews and Gentiles concerning faith in Christ. The Judaizers were trying to bring the Gentiles under the order of the tabernacle of Moses; they were insisting that right standing with God could only be obtained by means of the Law with its sacrificial systems and works. They were teaching about circumcision and Aaronic priesthood as part of what defined true followers of God. The fundamental question that was being asked at this council was, "What is the relationship of the Gentiles to the Mosaic covenant and the tabernacle of Moses?"

Peter stood up to testify about how he had seen the Lord pour out His Spirit on the Gentiles exactly as He had previously on the Jews at Pentecost; Paul and Barnabas corroborated his testimony (see Acts 15:7,12). After this, James quoted the prophecy of Amos concerning the restoration of the tabernacle of David, thereby showing that the purpose of this outpouring was, "So that the rest of mankind may seek the Lord, even all the Gentiles who are called by My name" (Acts 15:17). Throughout the worship order of David's tabernacle, the key of David will unlock the harvest and establish the Kingdom of God among the nations.

We are living in the last days, and the "fullness of the Gentiles" (Romans 11:25) is upon the Church. The Lord is raising up a people out of every tribe, tongue, kindred, and nation. According to Revelation 5:9-10, this remnant of believers shall stand before the throne of the Lamb singing new songs and playing instruments as they collectively worship Jesus after the order of David's tabernacle. In these last days, the Church must grasp the key of David—the key of worship—as never before. This is the key that unlocks the heavens. Believers need a baptism of discernment so they can sense the present season and understand what to do as demonic activity increases throughout the world and Church.

Worship is so much more than a Sunday morning event—it is a weapon of spiritual warfare and a key to the end-time harvest!

Chapter 13

BREAKING THE SOUND BARRIER

*Thou art worthy, O Lord, to receive glory
and honour and power: for thou hast created
all things, and for thy pleasure they are and
were created* (REVELATION 4:11 KJV).

With an understanding of the spiritual dynamics of worship and the emergence of the tabernacle of David in the last days, we are ready to look at the kind of worship God likes and at why it is so important to be concerned with His particular taste more than with our own. With all of the modern worship wars that debate style and taste, many Christians have never taken the time to gain insight from the Word concerning the kind of worship God Himself enjoys. The purpose of the believer's life is to bring the Lord pleasure! "Thou art worthy, O Lord, to receive glory and honour and power: for thou hast created all things, and for thy pleasure they are and were created" (Revelation 4:11 KJV). We should be more concerned with what the King desires and enjoys than with what we desire and enjoy. Worship is not about us. It is about Him.

When we make worship an earthbound, horizontal experience only, we remove power from worship. Worship should be primarily vertical in its expression. The purpose of worship is the connecting of earth with the heavens—deep calling unto deep. As was the cross, true worship is like a crucible, a place or situation in which different elements interact to produce something new.

Jesus said when He was asked about the most important commandment in the Scripture:

> *The first is, "Hear, O Israel: the Lord our God, the Lord is one; you shall love the Lord your God with all your heart, and with all your soul, and with all your mind, and with all your strength." The second is this, "You shall love your neighbor as yourself." There is no other commandment greater than these* (Mark 12:29-31 NRSV).

In other words, our vertical position of worship, which expresses our love for God, directly affects our horizontal position in life, which is to love our neighbor as we love ourselves. God has told His children, "Strive first for the kingdom of God and his righteousness, and all these things will be given to you as well" (Matthew 6:33 NRSV). Prayer and worship make the transaction possible; they bring Heaven down to earth.

DAY AND NIGHT WORSHIP

To discover what and how God desires worship, we must look to the tabernacle of David. As we have learned, David's tent was characterized by worship through songs and instruments, day and night. The tabernacle of David was a place of unceasing prayer, praise, and proclamation, and any study of the book of Psalms should penetrate far beyond the theological truths to include the realm of psalms as music. Most of the psalms in the book of Psalms were birthed in David's tent.

In the headers of the psalms, the names of three individuals appear consistently: Heman, Asaph, Jeduthun. First Chronicles chapters 15 and 16 identify these three men as the main directors of the Levitical ensembles. Heman was the lead singer. Asaph was the choir director. Jeduthun, also referred to as Ethan, was the musical director, the man who was in charge of the musical instruments. Each of them had his place in the tabernacle based on his specific anointing.

According to First Chronicles 16, Heman and Jeduthun were the leaders who were responsible for the sounding of the trumpets and cymbals and for the playing of the other instruments for sacred songs:

> *Every morning and evening they offered burnt offerings on the altar of burnt offerings, following the rules written in the Teachings of the Lord, which he had given Israel. With them were Heman and Jeduthun and other Levites. They were chosen by name to sing praises to the Lord because his love continues forever. Heman and Jeduthun also had the job of playing the trumpets and cymbals and other musical instruments when songs were sung to God...* (1 Chronicles 16:40-42 NCV).

The notation under the title of Psalm 88 attributes its authorship not to David, but rather to Heman the Ezrahite, calling it "a psalm of the sons of Korah." The name *Heman* means "faithful" in Hebrew.

Appropriate for someone who gathered the people to worship, the name *Asaph* means "God has gathered" in Hebrew. Twelve psalms (Psalm 50 and Psalms 73-83) carry the name *Asaph* at the beginning, and this can mean either that Asaph wrote them (or transcribed them for King David) or that they belong to a collection under his name and would have been performed in a certain style.

Skilled musicians and some lovers of music have noticed that certain songs seem to have more power in specific keys. Likewise, certain songs have different degrees of anointing based on the instruments or the vocalists involved. David understood this instinctively. He had a sense of sound, and he knew how to create it for particular situations or needs. He demonstrated this knowledge when his skillful harp-playing calmed the evil spirits that tormented King Saul: "And it came to pass, when the evil spirit from God was upon Saul, that David took an harp, and played with his hand: so Saul was refreshed, and was well, and the evil spirit departed from him" (1 Samuel 16:23 KJV). The sound of the harp music soothed Saul's spirit and repelled the demonic spirit that had assaulted him.

So we see that David had a unique understanding about the power of music, worship, and sound, and we can learn much from him.

POWER OF SOUND

Within the Body of Christ, little is understood about the power of sound. That is why I say that we need to "break the sound barrier" within the Church. Sound matters to God—specifically, the musical sounds attached to the worship of God.

David understood something about the power of a song when he used certain styles of music to produce a specific sound. As I have already noted in Chapter 12, the songs we know as the psalms carry notations that indicate what kinds of musical sounds best match with the words to make them pleasing to God.

God loves a harmonious noise! Take a look at this familiar picture of Heaven: "And I heard a voice from heaven, like the voice of many waters, and like the voice of loud thunder. And I heard the sound of harpists playing their harps. They sang as it were a new song before the throne, before the four living creatures, and the elders..." (Revelation 14:2-3). The volume and range of the sounds in Heaven probably rival the thundering power of Niagara Falls close up. If you have ever traveled to the base of Niagara Falls on one of those tour boats, you know that besides being very wet, it is very *loud* there. In fact, you can scream at someone next to you and they can't hear you. The water is crashing down and the air is too full of all of the possible sound frequencies already.

It will be just as loud in Heaven or louder, but at least nobody will need to ask questions or discuss anything anymore. Every frequency of sound will be occupied with lifting up the name of God. The angels will be flying to and fro as every tribe, tongue, kindred, and nation will be praising God forever and ever.

We must understand that God is not looking for just any sound; He's looking for *His* sound. He's looking for the sound that originates in Heaven, reflected back to Him by his worshipping people. Whenever we can find and reproduce that sound—and I do not mean one single note but any of an endless variety of notes and styles—God moves on the earth. That is how we get a little more of Heaven on earth.

The new Heaven and new earth will in the future once again become a place filled with the sounds of joyful worship:

> *And I saw a new heaven and a new earth: for the first heaven and the first earth were passed away; and there was no more sea. And I John saw the holy city, new Jerusalem, coming down from God out of heaven, prepared as a bride adorned for her husband. And I heard a great voice out of heaven saying, Behold, the tabernacle of God is with men, and he will dwell with them, and they shall be his people, and God himself shall be with them, and be their God* (Revelation 21:1-3 KJV).

SOUND THERAPY

Our instruments are tuned to "A-440" standard. This means that your eardrum picks up 440 pulses for the "A" note that is above middle

C. The human ear cannot pick up ultra-high-frequency sounds or extra-low-frequency sounds, although such sounds can have an unseen effect on your body. If you go low enough, you can only *feel* the sound as your heart skips a beat.

Genetic scientists have been using sound to code the proteins of living cells. By assigning a musical note to each protein instead of the more traditional letters of the alphabet, they can "play" the music and make comparisons. This is from a report titled, "Your DNA Is a Song: Scientists Use Music to Code Proteins," by John Roach in *National Geographic News* on October 21, 2005:

> All living things are made up of proteins. Each protein is a string of amino acids. There are 20 different amino acids, and each protein can consist of dozens to thousands of them.
>
> Scientists write down these amino acid sequences as series of text letters. Clark and her colleagues assign musical notes to the different values of the amino acids in each sequence. The result is music in the form of "protein songs."
>
> By listening to the songs, scientists and students alike can hear the structure of a protein. And when the songs of the same protein from different species are played together, their similarities and differences are apparent to the ear.
>
> "It's an illustration transferred into a medium people will find more accessible than just [text] sequences," Clark [Mary Anne Clark, a biologist at Texas Wesleyan University in Fort Worth] said. "If you look at protein sequences, if you just read those as they are written down, recorded in a database, it's hard to get a sense for the pattern."

In a similar set of experiments, when human genes are assigned specific notes, they seem to be playing a melody. When the music of a typical healthy strand of DNA is played, it sounds soothing and harmonic. On the other hand, a diseased strand of DNA grows more dissonant as its signal becomes less healthy. Scientists are using this technique to help discover and predict disease developments. Here is what one researcher discovered, as reported in "A Musical Score for Disease," by Jennifer Chu (in *Biomedicine News,* July 18, 2008):

> Gil Alterovitz, a research fellow at Harvard Medical School… is developing a computer program that translates protein and gene expression into music. In his acoustic translation, harmony represents good health, and discord indicates disease….
>
> Searching for a more simplified way to represent the complex library of information inherent in gene expression, Alterovitz decided to represent those changes with music. He hopes that doctors will one day be able to use his music to detect health-related changes in gene expression early via a musical slip into discord, potentially improving a patient's outcome.

Much as with sound therapy for the human body, God seems to be retuning the Body of Christ to the original sound of Heaven. Astronomers have even created the sounds of the universe (actually converted from X-ray signals). This brings to mind the words of one of David's psalms:

> *The heavens declare the glory of God, and the skies announce what his hands have made.*
>
> *Day after day they tell the story; night after night they tell it again. They have no speech or words; they have no voice to be heard. But their message goes out through all the world; their words go everywhere on earth…* (Psalm 19:1-4 NCV).

Think about it—Davidic worship always reappeared in every revival mentioned in the Old Testament. And every revival in world history engendered a specific sound or style of music that marked the moving of the Spirit. I believe that as the Church comes into more complete align-ment with the sounds of Heaven, there will be a mighty outpouring of God's Spirit in the earth. It appears that another revival of the sound of the tabernacle of David is being released in the earth today, and I want all of us to be part of it.

PSALMS, HYMNS, SPIRITUAL SONGS

The Church needs to break the sound barrier! There is a new sound that God desires to release in the Body of Christ right now. With the release of that new sound will come a fresh anointing that will break forth in a powerful revival.

As every worship leader prepares to lead worship, he needs to seek God about specific keys, colors, vocalists, instruments, and styles. All of these factors in combination are keys to releasing a sound that pleases the heart of God and produces a symphony between Heaven and earth. Just as we can choose to pray or sing in our native languages or we can pray or sing in tongues, so we can choose to make worshipful sounds with our own understanding or we can rely on the Holy Spirit to give us both words and tunes. When you speak out in prayerful words that are infused with the Spirit of God, you are singing a new song to Him. You are breaking off the power of old sounds, so to speak, and ushering in the heavenly sounds that bring healing and joy.

The Church needs to take worship out of the religious box and explore the sounds of the Spirit realm. Worship is not about a specific style or taste; it is about discovering what brings God pleasure. More than once in his epistles, Paul explains what authentic New Testament worship is; it consists of "psalms, hymns, and spiritual songs." Here are his words:

> ...Be filled with the Spirit, addressing one another in psalms
> and hymns and spiritual songs, singing and making melody
> to the Lord with all your heart, always and for everything

giving thanks in the name of our Lord Jesus Christ to God the Father (Ephesians 5:18-20 RSV).

Let the word of Christ dwell in you richly, teach and admonish one another in all wisdom, and sing psalms and hymns and spiritual songs with thankfulness in your hearts to God (Colossians 3:16 RSV).

The Hebrew origin of word *psalm* means "to strike or twang or pluck the notes on a musical instrument." This says to me that God likes musical instruments of all types. The word *hymn* is derived from the Greek word *humnos* which means "a sacred song or song of praise," including a song of praise for heroes and conquerors. This says to me that God likes it when we sing the old songs of the forefathers of our faith. The phrase *spiritual songs* in the Greek is *pneumatikos,* which relates to the human spirit, which serves as God's instrument or organ in an unrehearsed manner. God likes us to sing songs that are unrehearsed and spontaneous, inspired by the Holy Spirit, in the same way that He likes us to pray in the Spirit, as Paul teaches: "Pray in the Spirit at all times with all kinds of prayers" (Ephesians 6:18 NCV).

Until believers take worship out of the church box and pursue the pleasure of God as the highest aim of worship, the sound of Heaven can never be released in the earth. This why I say that the Church needs to break the sound barrier!

Chapter 14

NEW SOUNDS ADVANCE NEW LIFE

*Give ear, O my people, to my teaching; incline your
ears to the words of my mouth! I will open my mouth
in a parable; I will utter dark sayings from of old,
things that we have heard and known, that our
fathers have told us. We will not hide them from
their children, but tell to the coming generation the
glorious deeds of the Lord, and his might, and the
wonders which he has wrought* (PSALM 78:1-4 RSV).

The whole purpose of a coming generation is to praise the Lord; in
other words, to release a sound into the heavens. I believe that we are that
generation. Based on the obvious fact that a new sound of worship from
the people of God has preceded every great move of God, we must—if we
want to see another great move of God in these days—find the new sound
that has been reserved for this moment. Our generation is the forerunner

of a great move of God, and if we want to participate, we must draw the life of Heaven down to earth through our Heaven-inspired worship.

IT IS NEW

The Church has tended to greatly underestimate the power of sound, so much so that we have missed some of the sounds that God wanted to bring to the Church. We have allowed the devil to keep them in the world, stealing them and perverting them and taking our children into bondage. As you may have noticed, the Church always seems to be about twenty years behind the cutting edge of what the Spirit of God is doing in the earth. Whenever God begins to do something new, people react negatively to it, often deriding it and rendering it inactive in the Body of Christ simply because it's new. We prefer the old, familiar things, and we get suspicious of something new and unusual. If it doesn't sound like something we have heard before, we will put it in a box and label it "unscriptural" or "ungodly," only to find out ten years later we should have grabbed hold of that new sound. (By that time, of course, because we are already ten years behind and we will spend the next ten years trying to learn how to do the new thing, we will be twenty years behind by the time we get it down.)

We have been circling around this idea of reestablishing the tabernacle of David. James quoted the prophet Amos when he predicted to the leaders of the early church that the time was coming for the Church to restore the practice of day and night worship so that the glory of God would once again dwell with the people of God (see Acts 15:16). Davidic worship is not silent. It is not limited in scope. It is extravagant and it is loud—and it reflects back to Heaven the praise and adoration of God that originates in Heaven.

From the original tabernacle (tent) of David issued forth many sounds: the sounds of many kinds of instruments, singing voices, prophetic pronouncements, praise and thanksgiving, and declarations of truth. The psalms that we have collected in the Bible comprise David's Hit Parade of the songs that were written in the presence of God in the tabernacle. Every day it was a new sound, a new praise, a new declaration, a new prayer coming out from that place. The Bible says that as long as that sound went forth, David's enemies were at peace with him.

The actual tabernacle of David is long gone, but the glorious sounds of worship have been reintroduced by the Spirit in every generation in which the Church has experienced revival. Even from the early years of the Church that promise of revival has applied not only to Jews but also to Gentiles, non-Jews like us who belong to the Christian churches today. This is why we can take hold of this idea with both hands—the tabernacle of David belongs to us, too!

THE SOUND OF DAVIDIC WORSHIP

The Old Testament is filled with examples of how God brings victory, liberty, and revival to Israel after Davidic worship has been restored. One of the best examples can be found in the story of Nehemiah:

Now at the dedication of the wall of Jerusalem they sought out the Levites in all their places, to bring them to Jerusalem to celebrate the dedication with gladness, both with thanksgivings and singing, with cymbals and stringed instruments and harps. And the sons of the singers gathered together from the countryside around Jerusalem.... So I brought the leaders of Judah up on the wall, and appointed two large thanksgiving choirs.... ...Ezra the scribe went before them. By the Fountain Gate, in front of them, they went up the stairs of the City of David, on the stairway of the wall, beyond the house of David, as far as the Water Gate eastward. ...So the two thanksgiving choirs stood in the house of God, likewise I and the half of the rulers with me; and the priests, Eliakim, Maaseiah, Minjamin, Michaiah, Elioenai, Zechariah, and Hananiah, with trumpets; also Maaseiah, Shemaiah, Eleazar, Uzzi, Jehohanan, Malchijah, Elam, and Ezer. The singers sang loudly with Jezrahiah the director. Also that day they offered great sacrifices, and rejoiced, for God had made them rejoice with great joy; the women and the children also rejoiced, so that the joy of Jerusalem was heard afar off. ... Both the singers and the gatekeepers kept the charge of their God and the charge of the purification, according to the command of David and Solomon his son. For in the days of David and Asaph of old there were chiefs of the singers, and songs of praise and thanksgiving to God (Nehemiah 12:27-28,31,36-37,40-43,45-46).

Other Old Testament champions of effective corporate worship include Abijah (see 2 Chronicles 13:14-15), Asa (see 2 Chronicles 15:12-15), Jehoshaphat (see 2 Chronicles 20:18-22), Joash (see 2 Chronicles 23:12-15), Hezekiah (see 2 Chronicles 29:25-30), Josiah (see 2 Chronicles 35:15), and Zerubbabel (see Ezra 2:65-3:10-13). In every generation, the restoration of the sound of God in the earth brings with it the glory of His presence.

Starting on the day of Pentecost, Davidic worship once again returned, this time to the early church. We have seen ups and downs over the centuries since then, and I believe that we are currently in the middle of a time of increase. Once again we need to heed the advice of Paul in Ephesians 5:19 and Colossians 3:16 in which he urged the people of Ephesus and Colossae—and thereby every believer who would hear those words—to sing "psalms and hymns and spiritual songs" at all times. If we go back to this kind of worship, if we let God reestablish worship in us and if we find His new sound, then the presence of God will be released in a new way in our midst.

If we want to be part of a revival of biblical proportions, we need to seek the sound of Heaven that God wants to release in our generation. We should understand that God is not going to release a new sound only in one dimension; He will always release it in numerous dimensions. Thus, as we sing psalms, hymns, and spiritual songs, we find new ways to express our love and gratitude to God.

SONGS OF THE HEROES OF THE PAST

I am convinced of the importance of the old hymns in addition to David's psalms and new songs. We cannot rebuild from scratch in each generation; we need the benefit of the anointing of previous generations. We need the release of the old into the new.

In spite of plenty of preaching and teaching to the contrary, the book of Proverbs clearly states that we should not tear down the ancient landmarks. "Do not remove the ancient landmark, which your fathers have set" (see Proverbs 22:28 and Proverbs 23:10). Landmarks in the Spirit need to be renewed in each new generation.

Sometimes we need to sing "How Great Thou Art." We need to remember, "What can wash away my sin? Nothing but the blood of Jesus." We need to let our spirits soar with heavenly lyrics: "Holy, holy, holy; Lord, God Almighty!" "All hail the power of Jesus' name! Let angels prostrate fall; bring forth the royal diadem, and crown Him Lord of all."

Something about singing those old songs brings a fresh presence of God. For one thing, they remind us where we have come from. Those songs have stood the test of time. They need to be sung because they have worked; they have secured people's faith; they express stable doctrine. (Now I don't think that every single old song needs to be sung. Some of them are not even scriptural: "Just build me a cabin in the corner of Gloryland...." And I'm not advocating that we slip into worshipping the songs themselves, or the styles of music, which can happen, as evidenced by "worship wars.")

The Bible says that one generation will praise God to another generation: "One generation shall laud thy works to another, and shall declare thy mighty acts" (Psalm 145:4 RSV). This makes it possible for us to discover the sounds of a prior generation. The songs of heroes from days gone by will release the spirit of prophecy of that generation upon the people who sing their songs.

We are told that whenever a new high priest would be anointed in ancient Israel, they would purposely *not* provide him with a brand-new priestly garment. When the previous high priest's term of service came to an end and a new high priest was anointed, they would take the garments that had already been anointed from the most recent high priest and put them on the new priest and then they would pour fresh anointing oil on top of the old anointing. Thus the high priestly anointing was compounded from one priest to another, from one generation to the next.

This is something like what we do when we sing the old, already-anointed songs. God can add a new anointing to the old one, which is a powerful thing. The prophetic sound of the older generations can get released into the current generation. The combination of the old sound with a new one will increase the anointing, thus potentially making every generation more anointed than the generation before it.

HEARD ANY GOOD ODES LATELY?

When Paul endorsed the singing of spiritual songs, he used the Greek word *ode* for song. An ode follows a particular structure, and it usually has three parts, the *strophe,* and *antistrophe,* and the *epode.* A classical ode was usually also accompanied by instruments.

The word *strophe* implies turning one foot for the other or to the other, which indicates that a spiritual song makes your feet want to move, even to dance. The word *antistrophe* means to go the other way. In the midst of the music, you would have somebody over here doing one thing, and somebody over there doing something else. Then the *epode* part means "everybody go the same direction."

The early church followed this literally. Starting as early as the time of the writing of the New Testament, the Christians would put one group on one side and another group on the other and have the two choruses sing back and forth. This is almost like one generation declaring its praise to another, strophe to antistrophe. Call and response. Then they would all join together in singing the same song to Heaven (the epode). Part of their inspiration might have come from the sixth chapter of Isaiah, in which the activity of heavenly worship is being described. The seraphim (a special kind of angels) on one side of the throne of God cry out, "Holy!" and then the seraphim on the other side respond, "Holy!" Back and forth they cry out, until it all becomes one sound. In the same way, Christians' unrehearsed spiritual songs inspire movement in different directions. Then at a certain point, the unity of the Spirit will come upon the singers and all will start moving together.

NEW SOUNDS MAKE THINGS HAPPEN

In Chapter 1, I described three of the primary results of a new sound. Here is a summary:

1. New sounds break old cycles: Moses wrote new songs just before he led the people out of Egyptian captivity into the wilderness and again just before they entered the Promised Land, leaving the wilderness behind. The first one broke the cycle of captivity and the second broke the cycle of wandering in the wilderness.

2. New sounds release strategy: Gideon reactivated genuine worship and afterward God gave him a unique strategy for overcoming the Midianite army.

3. New sounds break the spirit of division: Gideon destroyed the Midianites whose very name means "strife and division."

New sounds matter greatly; they can affect major changes in both the spiritual and physical climate of a place.

Before Gideon tore down the altars of Baal and reestablished proper worship, he did not know what to do about the oppression of the Midianites. (The story is in the sixth and seventh chapters of the book of Judges.) God told him that in order to defeat the Midianites' large army (too large to count) he would need only three hundred handpicked soldiers. Three hundred? It seemed impossible. Yet with the God-ordained strategy, those three hundred men succeeded.

He gave each man an empty clay pitcher and had him shelter a burning torch inside. Each man also had a trumpet. Upon command, they were to shatter the clay pitchers, revealing the lights, and to blow a loud sound on their horns. Gideon would never have thought up this strategy on his own and if anyone besides God Himself had suggested it, he would have laughed it off. Yet, Gideon followed God's strategy to the letter, and it worked beautifully:

Gideon told the men, "Watch me and do what I do. When I get to the edge of the camp, do what I do. Surround the enemy camp. When I and everyone with me blow our trumpets, you blow your trumpets, too. Then shout, 'For the Lord and for Gideon!'" So Gideon and the one hundred men with him came to the edge of the enemy camp just after they had changed guards. It was during the middle watch of the night. Then Gideon and his men blew their trumpets and smashed their jars. All three groups of Gideon's men blew their trumpets and smashed their jars. They held the torches in their left hands and the trumpets in their right hands. Then they shouted, "A sword for the Lord and for Gideon!" Each of Gideon's men stayed in his place around the camp, but the Midianites began shouting and running to escape. When Gideon's three hundred men blew their trumpets, the Lord

made all the Midianites fight each other with their swords!
(Judges 7:17-22 NCV)

In the dead of the dark night, Gideon's men had crept up silently around the Midianite encampment. Usually only the captains of thousands possessed horns, so the enemy thought a vast army had surrounded them when they heard the three hundred horns. Besides, when they heard the breaking of the clay pots it sounded to their alarmed ears like the clashing of swords. They went crazy with confusion and fright. They freaked out. In the darkness, they turned on each other and annihilated themselves.

This brings me to a fourth important result of releasing God's new sound: *a new sound releases faith.* The sound of the clay pitchers breaking and the trumpets blowing inspired panic among the Midianites but exultant faith among the Israelites. In the same way, Joshua defeated Jericho not so much because of the loud shout but by faith: "By faith the walls of Jericho fell after they had been encircled for seven days" (Hebrews 11:30 NRSV).

Fifth, *a new sound releases the prophetic.* Revelation 19:10 (KJV) reads, "the testimony of Jesus is the spirit of prophecy," which indicates the connection. Prophecy is not some kind of mystical hooey; it is simply hearing God's words. A prophet knows what God is doing and saying. The best way to get in touch with the Spirit of God prophetically is to worship until you can walk right into the throne room.

You and I are mere "clay jars": "But we have this treasure in clay jars, so that it may be made clear that this extraordinary power belongs to God and does not come from us" (2 Corinthians 4:7 NRSV). It does not matter whether you are tall and I am short or whether we are rich or poor. What matters is our voice. When we release it in worship, we surrender ourselves to God. We break our clay pots open with praise, and we defeat the enemy without lifting one foot.

Our victory will never come until we get our clay vessels broken. We can either fight in our own insufficient strength and lose or we can win against all odds by letting God's light shine. Our God is an awesome God, worthy of every victory shout!

Chapter 15

HEAVEN AND EARTH RESONATING TOGETHER

The wind bloweth where it listeth, and thou hearest the sound thereof, but canst not tell whence it cometh, and whither it goeth: so is every one that is born of the Spirit (JOHN 3:8 KJV).

As God's Spirit moves across the earth, He is always looking for a responsive heart: "For the eyes of the Lord run to and fro throughout the whole earth, to show his might in behalf of those whose heart is blameless toward him" (2 Chronicles 16:9 RSV). He is looking for someone who will echo His heart in the earth. He wants to blow across a responsive person the way you might blow on an empty bottle causing a sound to resound from it. When He is active, something takes place on the earth that mirrors Heaven. As Jesus prayed: "Our Father which art in heaven, hallowed be thy name. Thy kingdom come, Thy will be done in earth, as it is in heaven" (Matthew 6:9-10 KJV). As you can see in chapters four and five of the book of Revelation, that resonating sound is a lot like Heaven.

The new Heaven and the new earth are going to include a restoration of that sound that is passing between Heaven and earth. It is a sound of worship. As a believer, you have been given authority to allow Heaven to invade the earth, but the only way you can do it is by making a Heaven-sent sound. When you echo the frequency of the Spirit of God, you will find that the sound breaks things in your life that need to be broken. Much like the breaking of a bottle of anointing oil, a new anointing gets released. Heaven invades. We can't contain it.

MAKE A JOYFUL NOISE TO THE LORD

God is waiting to hear a sound arising from this generation— Heaven to earth; earth back to Heaven; Heaven down to earth again, always resonating with power. When that heavenly sound is released, things happen. The Kingdom of God comes a little bit more into the earth as the people of God exercise their legal dominion over the earth.

We are far too weak in our own strength. Even an all-around athlete at the peak of his or her form or a person with a genius-level mind cannot bring Heaven to earth. But "the Spirit also helps in our weaknesses. For we do not know what we should pray for as we ought, but the Spirit Himself makes intercession for us with groanings which cannot be uttered" (Romans 8:26). Sometimes you get to the place that you don't know what words to say to God. It doesn't matter if you can only moan, as long as the sound originates from the Spirit of God. There is something powerful even in an "Oh…Oh…Oh, God!"

In fact, one of the most powerful prayer warriors I have ever known in my life is a man who said nothing but, "Oh, God! Oh, God!" for two hours straight. I was with him the whole time; that was all he said, but man, his moaning could get more miracles from the Lord than all of my wordy prayers. Something came out of his inner self that was like the Spirit of God blowing across his spirit as if he were an empty bottle. He didn't have to drum up the sound as you could do by thumping on the bottle. (Naturally, that would be an effective way to create sound with an empty bottle, but that's not the sound God is listening for. He wants to hear the resonant sound that His own Spirit makes when He blows over a responsive person or group of people.)

What happened on the day of Pentecost proves it:

> *And when the day of Pentecost was fully come, they were all with one accord in one place. And suddenly there came a sound from heaven as of a rushing mighty wind, and it filled all the house where they were sitting. And there appeared unto them cloven tongues like as of fire, and it sat upon each of them. And they were all filled with the Holy Ghost, and began to speak with other tongues, as the Spirit gave them utterance* (Acts 2:1-4).

MAKING AN IMPACT

The power of that sound reverberating through the atmosphere, coming from the breath of the Holy Spirit, releases something in the heavens that changes things on earth. What does it change? Notably, it changes governmental authority, righteousness, the creative order, and the enemy.

Here is how I know that there is an impact on governmental authority. The book of Revelation shows us twenty-four elders falling down at worship. (See Revelation 4:10.) And in Psalm 149, I see that ruling elders and kings fall down at worship for another reason:

> *Praise the Lord! Sing to the Lord a new song, his praise in the assembly of the faithful! For the Lord takes pleasure in his people; he adorns the humble with victory. Let the faithful*

exult in glory; let them sing for joy on their couches. Let the high praises of God be in their throats and two-edged swords in their hands, to wreak vengeance on the nations and chastisement on the peoples, to bind their kings with chains and their nobles with fetters of iron, to execute on them the judgment written! This is glory for all his faithful ones. Praise the Lord! (Psalm 149:1,4-9 RSV)

When the sound that comes out of the Body of Christ begins to resonate through the atmosphere of this earth, chains and fetters of iron limit the actions of world leaders. You may say, "I don't like the president's policies." Well, quit complaining about them and start praying instead. You will begin to see things line up with Heaven if you pray and worship with a heavenly voice. The president and others may never understand what is happening, but it will be almost like blowing a dog whistle; human hears can't hear it, but the dog lines up with what you want him to do. When the people of God release God's sound, it doesn't matter if they are Democrat, Republican, black, white, green, or yellow; something about the frequency of that sound of the Body of Christ in the spirit realm causes things to break and to be bound and loosed.

Whatever you bind on earth shall be bound in Heaven, and whatever you loose on earth will be loosed in Heaven (see Matthew 16:19). God says, "release a symphony on the earth and I will do something in the heavens that will reverberate back to the earth." The sound goes back and forth. Heaven echoes what we are echoing.

Then, we are changed. Those of us who have been redeemed, who are known as "the righteous," are broken anew and remade. When Isaiah stood in the courts of Heaven in the presence of heavenly worship stricken with awe, he became unraveled and undone: "Woe is me! I am lost, for I am a man of unclean lips, and I live among a people of unclean lips; yet my eyes have seen the King, the Lord of hosts!" (Isaiah 6:5 NRSV). He fell on his face overwhelmed by the sound of Heaven.

That sound has an impact on the creative order. The first disciples prayed, and the building was shaken with a divine earthquake (see Acts 4:31). In Second Chronicles 5:11-14, the trumpeters and singers joined in unison to give praise and thanks to God, accompanied by trumpets, cymbals, and other instruments. As they raised their voices in praise, singing, "He is good! His love endures forever!" the temple of the Lord was immediately filled with the glory cloud of God.

God created us to make a sound because it has an immediate impact on the enemy. God created us as praise instruments, holy noisemakers. Why else would an infant cry immediately after birth? That cry does something; it makes things happen. That's how we were created. If the cry of a mere baby puts things in motion, just think what a cry from the Body of Christ can accomplish.

God says, "Out of the mouth of babes and nursing infants You have ordained strength, because of Your enemies, that You may silence the enemy and the avenger" (Psalm 8:2). God created us to make a sound because of our enemies.

The devil can't stand to hear your voice releasing sound into the heavens in the form of praise to God because he knows all about its impact on the spirit realm and his demonic forces. He knows that such a sound can shut demonic forces down, and he knows that such a sound initiates the release of the glory of God into the earth.

It all comes out of a sound.

BREAKTHROUGH SOUNDS

I cannot emphasize enough that we must learn how to participate in God's symphony of sound. Several Hebrew words for praise help us understand more about it.

The first one is *zamar*. One place this word can be found is in this passage from the book of Judges: "Hear, O kings! Give ear, O princes! I, even I, will sing to the Lord; I will sing praise to the Lord God of

Israel" (Judges 5:3). Other versions substitute the phrase *make melody* for *sing praise*, because the word *zamar* means "to praise by singing." This is quoted from the song of Deborah as she stood with the Israelites when they were under their enemy's attack. No enemy threat was going to prevent Deborah from singing her praises of God!

The second word is *barak*. It is used frequently in the Old Testament, and here is a familiar example from the psalms: "Bless the Lord, O my soul: and all that is within me, bless his holy name. Bless the Lord, O my soul, and forget not all his benefits" (Psalm 103:1-2 KJV). *Barak* means "to kneel down," specifically to kneel in order to speak about someone's excellence. It does not mean merely the action of kneeling; it means kneeling coupled with telling someone how praiseworthy he or she is. In the psalm, the psalmist is saying, "You are excellent, O God, and You are worthy. Everything in me bows down before Your excellence." *Barak* is a sound of praise that occurs along with a change of posture.

A third Hebrew word for praise is *towdah*. Like *barak,* this word appears often in the Old Testament, and it means "to thank God by means of a sacrifice of confession, opening your mouth in praise with personal gratitude to God." Here is a good example from the book of Leviticus: "And when you sacrifice a sacrifice of thanksgiving to the Lord, you shall sacrifice it so that you may be accepted" (Leviticus 22:29 RSV).

In the temple, when an animal sacrifice was made this was the word that was used. When they killed the sacrificial lamb or red heifer and the beast would cry out with a bleat or a bellow, the worshippers would say, *"Towdah!"* The sacrifice expressed their worship of God.

Our lives can be painful sometimes, yet praising God out of the midst of the pain, as sacrificial as it may be, puts you in the position of an overcomer. We refuse to let pain control our praise. Our praise controls our pain, not the other way around. It is *towdah* when I confess God's greatness in the middle of my pain.

When their brother Lazarus died, Mary and Martha were in the extreme pain of grief. Jesus arrived, and Martha met him, saying to Him, "Lord, if you had been here, my brother would not have died" (John 11:21 NCV). He replied, "Just believe." Of course, that was not easy. Lazarus had been dead already for four days. "By now, there will be a stench," said practical Martha. She had been going into the tomb every day for the first three days after his death, anointing her brother's body. The Jews believed that after three days the dead person's spirit completely leaves the body and the surrounding area and that there is no longer any hope whatsoever of a resurrection. Here it was the fourth day, and the tomb had been sealed.

Jesus told them to unseal it, saying, "I am the resurrection and the life" (see John 11:25). Then He walked up to the entrance of the tomb and commanded: "Lazarus, come forth!" The sound of His voice went through rock, passed by every dead body already in the tomb, penetrated the stench, and went right to Lazarus' body. His body, which had been created to respond to the voice of the Lord, the sound of Heaven, began to vibrate. Lazarus stood up in his grave wrappings and moved toward the unsealed entrance. Whenever you release praise and belief in the painful places of life *(towdah),* the resurrection power of God becomes available to you.

Another Hebrew word for praise is *shabach.* I like the sound of that word. It appears in Psalm 145:4—"One generation shall praise [*shabach*] Your works to another, and shall declare Your mighty acts." *Shabach* means, "because your love is better than life, my lips will glorify you" (see Psalm 63:3). A *shabach* is a shout. It is not just any old shout. It is a shout of address. It is saying, "Jesus! You *go,* Man!" Some things won't happen until somebody shouts like that.

Last but not least, we have the word *tehillah.* This word is used in Psalm 71:8 (NRSV), "My mouth is filled with your praise [*tehillah*], and with your glory all day long." The same word is used in Isaiah 61:3

(KJV), the verse that tells us to comfort those who mourn in Zion, to give them beauty instead of ashes, the oil of joy instead of mourning, and "the garment of praise [*tehillah*] for the spirit of heaviness."

Tehillah is a spiritual, spontaneous kind of worship that arises from your spirit when it has been stirred by the Lord's Spirit. As you begin to reach out to God, His Spirit begins to invade your spirit. The next thing you know, you are worshipping. It is unpredictable, and that is part of its power. Demonic forces of depression start breaking, and darkness shatters.

It is important to realize that praise and worship can take so many forms—*zamar, barak, towdah, shabach, tehillah*—and much more. It is even more important to turn your heart to give God praise at all times, the sounds of your worship echoing the sounds from Heaven.

LET'S WORSHIP IN DAVID'S TABERNACLE

Wherever the sound of worship rings out loud and clear, day and night, the tabernacle of David is restored. That sound slams into the powers of darkness and releases the light of Heaven. More than that, it brings the rule of Heaven right into the earth, where it belongs:

> *The heavens are Yours, the earth also is Yours;*
> *The world and all its fullness, You have founded them.*
> *The north and the south, You have created them....*
> *You have a mighty arm;*
> *Strong is Your hand, and high is Your right hand.*
> *Righteousness and justice are the foundation of Your throne;*
> *Mercy and truth go before Your face.*
> *Blessed are the people who know the joyful sound!*
> *They walk, O Lord, in the light of Your countenance.*
> *In Your name they rejoice all day long,*
> *And in Your righteousness they are exalted.*
> *For You are the glory of their strength,*

And in Your favor our horn is exalted.
For our shield belongs to the Lord,
And our king to the Holy One of Israel (Psalm 89:11-18).

Blessed indeed are the people who know how to release the joyful sound of Heaven. They know the power of it. They know they were created to worship their heavenly Father, joining their voices with many others.

Is your voice one of them? The time is always right for this sound of Heaven, and right now the symphony of praise is tuning up again. Can you hear it? Come and join your voice with mine in the high praises of our God!

DEDICATION

I dedicate this book to my loving wife Pam and my son Adam. Thank you for believing in me and supporting the call of God upon my life. My greatest victory is not the size of my ministry. The ultimate achievement of my life is serving the eternal God alongside of my beautiful family!

ABOUT THE AUTHOR

For more information about Pastor Shane Warren, resources, and how to invite him to speak contact:

Shane Warren Ministries
715 Cypress St.
West Monroe, La. 71291
Website:
www.shanewarren.org
Email: info@shanewarren.org
Phone: 318-387-1500

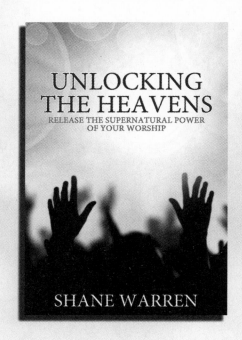